THAILAND
• AT COST •

A TRAVELLER'S GUIDE

LITTLE HILLS PRESS

We gratefully acknowledge the assistance of Fiona Ball of the Tourism Authority of Thailand.

Maps by Angela and Mark Butler

© Photographs — Tourism Authority of Thailand, Sydney
© Maps — Little Hills Press, 1990
© Map p. 4: Tourism Authority of Thailand

Editor: Fay Smith
Contributors: Christopher Ernest
　　　　　　　Oliver Koehler

Cover by Stuart Williams
Typeset and printed in Singapore by Singapore National Printers Ltd

© Little Hills Press, Revised edition 1990.
　　First printed 1989.
ISBN 1 86315 016 1

Little Hills Press Pty. Ltd.,
Tavistock House, 34 Bromham Road,
Bedford MK40 2QD,
United Kingdom.

Regent House,
37–43 Alexander Street,
Crows Nest NSW 2065 Australia.

Distributed in USA and Canada by
The Talman Company, Inc
150 Fifth Avenue
New York NY 10011 USA

DISCLAIMER

Whilst all care has been taken by the publisher and authors to ensure that the information is accurate and up to date, the publisher does not take responsiblity for the information published herein. As things get better or worse, places close and others open, some elements in the book may be inaccurate when you get there. Please write and tell us about it so we can update in subsequent editions.

CONTENTS

ROUTE MAP OF THAILAND

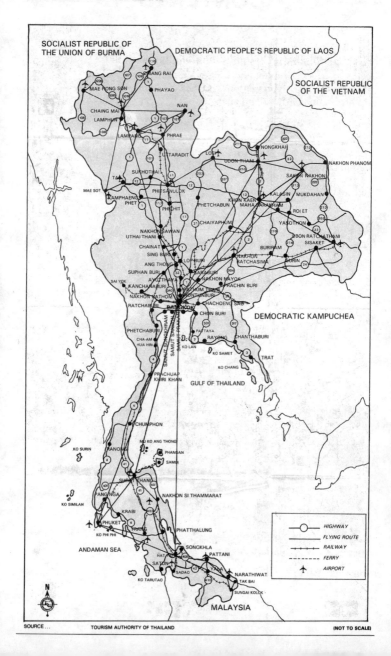

THAILAND

Located in South-East Asia, the Kingdom of Thailand is bordered by Burma to the west and north, Laos to the north-east, Kampuchea to the west, and Malaysia to the south. The country is approximately the same size as France, and has an area of some 500,000 km² (approx. 193,000 sq miles).

Thailand is divided into five distinct regions: the *mountainous north* where elephants work forests and winter temperatures are sufficiently cool to permit the cultivation of temperate fruits such as strawberries and peaches; the sprawling *north-east plateau*, largely bordered by the Mekong River, where the world's oldest Bronze Age civilisation flourished some 5,600 years ago; the *central plain*, one of the world's most fertile rice and fruit-growing areas; the *eastern coastal plain*, where the tourist beach resorts are situated; western mountains and valleys, suitable for the development of hydro-electric power; and the *peninsular south* with its diverse scenery and tin mining, rubber cultivation and fishing activities.

HISTORY

Archaeological discoveries near the north-east hamlet of Ban Chiang suggest that the oldest Bronze Age civilisation was alive and well in Thailand 5,600 years ago.

Successive waves of immigrants, including Mons, Khmers and Thais, gradually entered the land mass then known as Siam, most slowly travelling along fertile river valleys from southern China. By the 11th and 12th centuries, Khmers ruled much of the area from Angkor.

By the early 1200s, Thais had established small northern city states in Lana, Phayao and Sukhothai. In 1238, two Thai chieftains rebelled against Khmer rule and established the first truly independent Thai kingdom in Sukhothaik (literally, "Dawn of Happiness").

Sukhothai saw the Thais' gradual expansion throughout the entire Chao Phraya River basin, the establishment of Theravada Buddhism as the paramount religion, the creation of the Thai alphabet and the first expression of nascent Thai art forms, including painting, sculpture, architecture and literature.

The 1300s saw the decline of Sukhothai, which eventually became a vassal state of Ayutthaya, a young kingdom further south in the Chao Phraya river valley. Founded in 1350, Ayutthaya remained the capital until 1767 when it was destroyed by invaders from Burma.

During Ayutthaya's 417 years as the capital, under the rule of 33 kings, the Thais brought their distinctive culture to fruition, totally rid their lands of Khmer presence, and fostered contact with Arabian, Indian, Chinese, Japanese and European powers.

Ayutthaya's destruction was a severe blow to the Thais, however a revival occurred within a few months and the Burmese were expelled by King Taksin who later made Thon Buri his capital. In 1782, the first king of the present Chakri dynasty, Rama I, established his new capital on the site of a riverside hamlet called Ban Kok (Village of Wild Plums). In 1939, the name of the country was altered to Thailand.

Since World War II, the army has controlled the government for all but a few brief periods of civilian rule.

Today, Thailand is a constitutional monarchy. Since 1932, Thai kings, including the present monarch, HM King Bhumibol Adulyadej (Rama IX), have exercised their legislative powers through a national assembly, their executive powers through a cabinet headed by a prime minister, and their judicial powers through the law courts.

CLIMATE

Thailand has two distinct climates: a tropical savanna climate in most parts of the country, and a tropical monsoon climate in the southern and south-eastern regions. There are three well-defined seasons — the Hot Season (March through May), the Rains Season (June through October), and the Cool Season (November through February).

Average temperatures are about 27C (81F), ranging, in Bangkok for example, from 29C (84F) in April to 25C (77F) in December.

POPULATION

The people living in Thailand today share a rich ethnic diversity — mainly Thai, Mon, Khmer, Laotian, Chinese, Malay, Persian and Indian stock — with the result that there is no typically Thai appearance. There are small Thais, tall Thais, dark-skinned Thais and light-skinned Thais.

About 80% of the population is connected in some way with agriculture which, in varying degrees, influences, and is influenced by, the religious ceremonies and festivals that help make Thailand such a distinctive country.

LANGUAGE

Spoken and written Thai remain largely incomprehensible to the casual visitor. However, English is widely understood, particularly in Bangkok where it is almost the second commercial language. English is also spoken in most hotels, shops and restaurants, and in major tourist destinations.

There is a shortage of English language street signs in Bangkok, and the following might be useful to help you find your way around.

1	neung	18	sip peat
2	song	19	sip kao
3	sam	20	yi sip
4	si	30	sam sip
5	ha	40	si sip
6	hok	50	ha sip
7	chet	60	hok sip
8	paet	70	chet sip
9	kao	80	paet sip
10	sip	90	kao sip
11	sip et	100	neung roi
12	sip song	200	song roi
13	sip sam	300	sam roi
14	sip si	400	si roi
15	sip ha	500	ha roi
16	sip hok	600	hok roi
17	sip chet	700	chet roi

800 paet roi	2,000 song phan
900 kao roi	3,000 sam phan
1,000 phan	4,000 si phan

RELIGION

Theravada Buddhism is the professed religion of more than 90% of all Thais, and it has a strong influence on daily life.

Buddhism first appeared in Thailand during the 3rd Century BC at Nakhon Pathom, site of the world's tallest Buddhist monument, after the Indian Buddhist Emperor Asoka (267–227 BC) sent missionaries to South-East Asia to spread the newly established faith.

One reason for Buddhism's strength is that there are few Thai Buddhist families in which at least one member has not studied the Buddha's teachings in monastic surroundings. It has long been a custom for males over 20 to be temporarily ordained as monks for periods ranging from 3 days to 3 months. This usually occurs during the annual Rains Retreat, a 3-month period during the rainy season when all monks stay inside their monasteries. Also, it is not uncommon for Thai men, after discharging their family obligations, to spend the remainder of their lives as monks.

The Thai people have always subscribed to the ideal of religious freedom, and sizable minorities of Muslims, Christians, Hindus and Sikhs pursue their respective faiths unopposed.

FESTIVALS AND HOLIDAYS

Most festivals are connected either with religion, the annual rice-farming cycle, or honour Thai kings. Some occur on fixed dates, while those associated with Buddhism are determined by the lunar calendar. Many are also national holidays.

Makha Bucha — full-moon day, February — National Holiday
This commemorates the time when 1,250 disciples gathered to hear the Buddha preach. Offering food to monks and freeing captive birds and fish is interspersed with sermons throughout the day. Throughout the kingdom, after sunset, Buddhist monks lead the laity in a candlelight procession around chapels.

Flower Festival — second Friday, Saturday and Sunday in February
This annual event, celebrated in Chiang Mai, 700 km (434 miles) north of Bangkok, features displays, floral floats and beauty contests, at a time when the province's flowers are all in full bloom.

Phra Budda Baht Festival — February
Held at the Shrine of the Buddha's Footprint north of Saraburi.

Pattaya Festival — early April
Thailand's premier beach resort celebrates with beauty parades, floral floats, and special events. Highlights include a spectacular beachside firework display.

Chakri Day — April 6 — National Holiday
Commemorates the founding of the present Chakri Dynasty. Thailand's present monarch, HM King Bhumibol Adulyadej, is the ninth Chakri king.

Songkran Festival — April 13 — National Holiday
Once the traditional Thai New Year, Songkran is celebrated with special elan in Chiang Mai where it becomes a three-day carousel of socialising and good-natured water throwing.

Royal Ploughing Ceremony — usually early May
This ceremony marks official commencement of the annual rice-planting cycle. Presided over by His Majesty the King, elaborate Brahman ritual and ceremonies combine to provide predictions concerning the forthcoming crop.

Coronation Day — May 5 — National Holiday
Celebrates the coronation of King Bhumibol Adulyadej in 1950.

Wisakha Bucha — full-moon day, May — National Holiday
This is the holiest of all Buddhist days, marking the Buddha's birth, enlightenment and death.

Skyrocket Festival — second weekend in May
Held prior to the annual monsoon, north-east villagers build gigantic rockets to fire into the sky to ensure' bountiful rains. It is a traditional period for letting off steam before rice cultivation begins in earnest.

Asanhabucha — full-moon day, July — National Holiday
Marks the Buddha's first sermon to his first five disciples, and introduces 'Khao Phansa', the annual three-month Rains Retreat when all Buddhist monks stay inside their monasteries to study and meditate.

HM The Queen's Birthday — August 12 — National Holiday
Nationwide celebrations find particular focus in Bangkok, where government buildings are decorated and illuminated at night with coloured lights.

OK Phansa — usually October
Celebrates the end of Phansa and introduces the Kathin period when the Buddhist laity present monks with new robes and other items deemed necessary for the monkhood's upkeep during the forthcoming monastic year. The Kathin period also marks the official end of the Rainy Season, which is celebrated with country fairs, many of which feature regattas. Nan, 790 km (490 miles) north of Bangkok, has famous boat races, and other noteworthy regattas are held in Surat Thani, Phichit, Nakhon Phanom and Pathumthani.

Vegetarian Festival — during October
Phuket islanders of Chinese ancestry commit themselves to a vegetarian diet for 9 days. The festival's first day features a parade of white-clothed devotees and several ascetic displays.

Chulalongkorn Day — October 23 — National Holiday
Honours Thailand's most beloved king. Many people from all walks of life lay wreaths at his statue in Bangkok's Royal Plaza.

November marks the beginning of the Cool Season, coincides with low farming activity and is the time for innumerable temple fairs. The best known are Bangkok's Golden Mount Fair and the Phra Pathom Chedi Fair at Nakhon Pathom.

Loi Krathong — full-moon night, November
This is Thailand's loveliest festival when, under the full moon, Krathongs' (small lotus-shaped banana-leaf boats) are floated on the rivers and waterways. The little boats contain a lighted candle, glowing incense, a flower and a small coin to honour the water spirits and to wash away the past year's sins.

Elephant Round-Up — third weekend in November
In Surin, north-east Thailand, some 100 elephants participate in this popular event. Besides folk dances and traditional cultural performances, these versatile behemoths star in displays of time-honoured wild elephant hunts, demonstrations of intelligence, strength, gentleness and obedience. There is a spectacular re-enactment of a medieval war elephant parade.

River Kwai Bridge Week — late November/early December
Features a brilliant light and sound show at the world-famous bridge in Kanchanaburi, western Thailand. Archaeological and historical exhibitions, folk culture performances and rides on trains hauled by World War II vintage steam locomotives number among other attractions.

HM The King's Birthday — December 5 — National Holiday
On December 3, the elite Royal Guards swear anew allegiance to the King in Bangkok's Royal Plaza. This precedes the King's birthday, two days later, when festivities occur throughout the kingdom.

Constitution Day — December 10 — National Holiday
The year's last national holiday is mostly devoted to private celebrations.

ENTRY REGULATIONS
All visitors entering Thailand must have a valid passport. Visitors with confirmed onward tickets are allowed to stay in Thailand for a period of 15 days without a visa. For stays up to 30 days a Transit Visa is required; for 60 days, a Tourist Visa; and for 90 days, a Non-Immigrant Visa. Visas are obtainable from all Thai embassies and consulates, and visa extensions may be sought at the Immigration Division, Soi Suanphlu, Bangkok 10120 — fee does not exceed 500 baht.

NOTE: Please check the period of stay stamped in your passport by the immigration officer.

Narcotic drugs, pornographic material and firearms are strictly prohibited. Visitors may bring in any amount of foreign currency for their personal use, but amounts taken out may never exceed those declared upon entry. Visitors should note that there is a limit of 2,000 baht (Thai currency) per person they may bring into Thailand, and a limit of 500 baht per person of Thai currency they may take out of Thailand.

No innoculations or vaccinations are required unless you are coming from or passing through contaminated areas. Please check the latest regulations with your local Health Office.

COMMENT: Customs checks at Bangkok's Don Muang airport are very strict. On my last visit, officials were taking people out of the queues at random for, what we presumed to be, body searches. No-one was brave enough to question the people in charge. There are warning signs everywhere about drug-trafficking, and you only have to read your daily newspapers to know that these are not idle threats.

EMBASSIES

Australia	:	37 South Sathorn Road, Bangkok 10120, ph 286 0411.
New Zealand:		93 Wireless Road, Bangkok, ph 251 8165.
UK	:	Wireless Road, Bangkok, ph 253 0191.
USA	:	95 Wireless Road, Bangkok, ph 252 5040.
Canada	:	Boonmitre Bldg, 138 Silom Road, Bangkok, ph 234 1561.

MONEY

The Thai unit of currency is the baht, which is divided into 100 Satang. "Copper" coins are in denominations of 25 and 50 satang, "silver" coins in 1 and 5 baht. Bank notes are 10 baht (brown), 20 baht (green), 50 baht (blue), 100 baht (red) and 500 baht (purple).

Approximate exchange rates are:

A$	=	20.17 baht
NZ$	=	16.00
UK£	=	42.50
US$	=	25.40
Can$	=	23.00

US dollar traveller cheques can be conveniently cashed at all provincial banks and authorised money changers. Traveller cheques in other currencies are best changed in Bangkok where better rates prevail. Generally, hotel exchange rates are lower than those offered by banks and authorised money changers.

Thai and foreign banks provide standard services nationwide, Mon–Fri, except public and bank holidays, 8.30am–3.30pm. Bank currency exchange centres operate 7am–9pm, seven days a week, including holidays.

COMMUNICATIONS

To use Thailand's domestic telephone service, it is advisable to have hotel operators dial required numbers. Public telephones are not always reliable. However, international telephone calls are efficient, clear and can be made from Bangkok's Central GPO on New Road at any time of the day or night.

International Direct Dialling is available, and the Country Code is 66.

There are three English-language newspapers — Nation Review, Bangkok Post (morning) and Bangkok World (evening). Several English-language magazines are available at hotel newsagents, supermarkets, department stores and leading bookstores.

AM radio is heavily commercial, and there are around 200 stations. FM radio offers popular music, classical music, jazz, English-language news broadcasts, and the original soundtracks of certain imported films shown on local television's four commercial channels.

MISCELLANEOUS

Local time is GMT + 7.

Electricity supply is 220 volt, 50-cycle AC power.

Major international credit cards, such as American Express, Diners Club and VISA are accepted by major banks, restaurants, hotels and shops.

Business Hours

Most commercial concerns in Bangkok operate on a 5-day week. Government offices are generally open 8.30am–4.30pm, with noon–1pm lunchbreak, Mon–Fri. Private businesses maintain much the same hours, perhaps 8am–5pm with certain exceptions. Many stores open 12 hours a day, 7 days a week.

Airport Facilities
There is a duty-free shop, car hire (Avis, Hertz, Sin Tat Rent-A-Car), 24 hour banking and exchange facilities, and a 24 hour restaurant and bar in the departure lounge.

Departure Tax
There is a departure tax of 200 baht per person for international flights, and 20 baht for domestic flights.

Bargaining
Except in department stores where items have fixed prices, bargaining is an accepted practice throughout Thailand. Do not be embarrassed to ask for a discount or a large reduction when shopping for gemstones, antiques or handicrafts, or when hiring boats or sports equipment.

Church Services
Christian churches are found in Bangkok and most provincial capitals. Services are mostly in Thai, with certain services in English, French and German. Local English-language newspapers provide comprehensive listings of services in Bangkok.

Clothing
Light, loose cotton clothes are best. Nylon should be avoided. Sweaters are needed during the cool season evenings, or if visiting mountainous areas or remote national parks. Jackets and ties are required in certain restaurants and nightclubs.

Photography
Major international film manufacturers maintain photofinishing laboratories. Popular brands of film are available countrywide and 'still' photographers are free to shoot almost everything. Movie cameras are not allowed without permission in Bangkok's Grand Palace and Emerald Buddha Chapel complex. Photography is also prohibited in certain branches of the National Museum, which are found throughout the country.

Health
All tourism destinations and provincial capitals have hospitals and clinics staffed by trained doctors and nurses.

All water should be boiled before use, however bottled water is widely available. Don't fall into the trap of carefully not drinking the water out of the tap, but then cleaning your teeth at the sink, or ordering your scotch on the rocks. Salad vegetables should also be avoided in restaurants as, of course, they have probably been washed in the local water.

Milk, in all of Thailand, is unpasteurized, and should be boiled. Powdered and tinned milk is available, but make sure it is reconstituted with boiled water, otherwise you will be back where you started from.

Precautions are advised against Cholera, Typhoid and Malaria. It is advisable to check with your local doctor before you leave on your trip as to the type of medication best suited.

Etiquette

Polite behaviour is welcomed everywhere, and what is considered polite in other countries is probably considered polite in Thailand.

However, there are a few cultural pitfalls, mainly social and religious taboos, the breaking of which can cause offence:

* Thais revere their royal family. Even social malcontents who ignore legal and community standards refuse to tolerate a faintly implied slight on the Thai monarchy.
* Outward expressions of anger are regarded as crude and boorish. The visitor who remains calm and smiles appreciatively will find all sorts of doors open to him.
* Thais customarily ask each other questions which are regarded as being personal. If the visitor is asked, "Where are you going?" or "How much do you earn?" such questions are asked in a friendly manner and signify genuine interest. Joking answers such as "I'm not sure," or "Never enough!" are perfectly acceptable.
* Visitors should dress neatly in all religious shrines. They should never go shirtless, or in shorts, and ladies, shoulders must be covered.
* Shoes should be removed when entering private Thai homes; chapels where Buddhist images are kept; and any of the Islamic community's mosques.
* Each Buddha image, large or small, ruined or not, is regarded as being a sacred object. Never climb onto one to take a photograph or do anything that might show lack of respect.

* Public displays of affection between men and women are frowned upon. Westernised Thai couples may hold hands, but that's as far as it goes in polite society.
* It is considered rude to point your foot at a person or object.
* Thais regard the head as the highest part of the body, both literally and figuratively. Therefore, they do not appreciate anyone patting them there, even as a friendly gesture.

Tipping

It is not necessary to tip taxi drivers and cinema ushers, but it is customary to tip hotel personnel who have given good personal service. A 10% tip is appreciated in restaurants, particularly where the service charge is waived.

Emergencies

Bi-lingual Tourist Police are attached to Tourism Authority of Thailand offices in Bangkok, Pattaya, Chiang Mai, Hat Yai, Phuket and Kanchanaburi to provide speedy assistance to visitors.

Security for Patrons

 The emblem of Standard is issued by the Tourism Authority of Thailand to souvenir shops, restaurants and foodshops certifying to their standard and services. These are the places to be patronised.

Bang Pa-In, Ayutthaya, Thailand's ancient Capital

Bangkok, with its Monument to Democracy

Protector of the Temple

Dragon Dance for Chinese New Year, Nakhon Sawan

Thai Boxing

A Temple in Bangkok

TRAVEL INFORMATION

HOW TO GET THERE

By Air

Qantas has flights to Bangkok, via Singapore, from —
 Brisbane — 2 flights a week.
 Melbourne — 3 flights a week.
 Sydney — 3 flights a week.
 Perth — 1 flights a week.
 Adelaide — 3 flights a week (via Melbourne).
 Auckland — 3 flights a week (via Sydney).
         1 flight a week via Singapore.
 Christchurch — 1 flight a week (via Melbourne).
 Wellington — 2 flights a week (via Melbourne).

Qantas stops in Bangkok on its flight from London to Sydney/
Melbourne, and also has flights from San Francisco and Los
Angeles, via Sydney and Singapore, to Bangkok.

Thai International has flights to Bangkok from —
 Brisbane — 1 flight a week, via Singapore.
 Melbourne — 3 flights a week, via Singapore.
 Sydney — 4 flights a week, via Singapore.
 Perth — 1 flight a week, via Singapore.
 London — 6 flights a week, via Frankfurt, Copenhagen or
  Delhi.
 Toronto — 2 flights a week, via Tokyo.
 Dallas — 4 flights a week, via Tokyo.
 Seattle — 4 flights a week, via Tokyo.
 Auckland — 2 fights a week, via Singapore.
 Christchurch — 1 flight a week, via Singapore.

Singapore Airlines have flights to Bangkok, via Singapore, from —
 Adelaide — 3 flights a week.
 Brisbane — 5 flights a week.

Melbourne — 5 flights a week.
Perth — 2 flights a week.
Sydney — 5 flights a week.
Auckland — 2 flights a week.
Christchurch — 1 flight a week.

Cathay Pacific has flights to Bangkok, via Hong Kong, from —
Sydney — daily flights.
Melbourne — 6 flights a week.
Brisbane — 1 flight a week.
Perth — 1 flight a week.
San Francisco and Vancouver — daily flights, arriving Hong Kong for an overnight stay (8pm) with connecting flight next morning (9am) to Bangkok.

Northwest Airlines have daily flights from 8 cities in the United States, via Tokyo to Bangkok. British Airways have 4 flights a week from London to Bangkok direct.

Bangkok International Airport (Don Muang) is 25 km (15.5 miles) north of the city. There is an airport bus service to the City Terminal (Hotel Asia) every half hour between 6am–9pm.

A coach service is also available from the airport to Pattaya at 11am and 9pm, returning at 6am and 4pm.

By Sea

There are no regular steamship connections with Thailand. Cargo ships calling at Bangkok's Khlong Toei port sometimes have passenger cabin facilities. Cruise ships, such as Cunard's Queen Elizabeth II, periodically visit Pattaya.

By Rail

Regular rail services link Singapore and Bangkok. Intermediary stops include Kuala Lumpur, Butterworth and major southern Thai towns.

By Road

Overland entrance to Thailand is restricted to three road crossings on the Thai-Malaysian border, at Satun, Sadao and Betong.

PACKAGE TOURS

All the airlines offer package tours to Thailand, usually with either Singapore or Hong Kong included, and you should check with your travel agent as to the latest on offer.

As always these tours represent a great saving in accommodation, and also allow in most cases for internal flights and transfers to and from the various airports, which can take a lot of worry out of planning your holiday.

For example, Swingaway offer 6 days/5 nights package to Bangkok from Sydney and Melbourne, staying at the Royal Orchid Sheraton with return flights by Thai Airways for A$1,636 twin share. You can add to that 3 nights at the Royal Garden Resort in Pattaya for an extra A$101, or 5 nights at the Coral Beach Hotel on Phuket for A$359.

Singapore Airlines have a 12 days/10 nights package that takes in Singapore, Bangkok and Chiang Mai, for a high season (November — January) price of A$2,029 twin share, including return airfare. Hotels in this package are the Marco Polo in Singapore, Novotel in Bangkok and the Chiang Mai Orchid.

Cathay Pacific have Stay-A-While accommodation packages in Bangkok, which include full breakfast and return transfers between airport and hotel. For instance they offer a twin room in the Regent Bangkok for A$136 per person for the first night, and A$116 per person for extra nights. The duration of the stay is limited to 10 nights.

There are also fly/cruise tours available from different companies, such as Pearl Cruises, ph Sydney 261 8576. They offer 14 day Singapore, Bangkok, Bali and Beyond cruises, starting from A$4,650 per person twin share, including return air fares from Sydney, Melbourne or Brisbane.

TOURIST INFORMATION
The Tourism Authority of Thailand has its head office in Ratchadamnoen Nok Avenue, Bangkok 10100, Thailand, ph 282 1143–7. There are also branch offices throughout the country, and information on these will be included in the section pertaining to the area.

ACCOMMODATION
Thailand has world-class accommodation which is probably unsurpassed in terms of attentiveness, courteous service and affordability.

Major tourist destinations such as Bangkok, Pattaya, Chiang Mai and Phuket, offer modern first-class hotels, with international-standard convention facilities for groups numbering from 200 to 2,000 and upwards.

Family-style hotels, bungalow complexes, guest houses, house-boats, hostels, motels, spartan but clean Chinese-style inns and hotels and beachside huts complete a range of accommodation costing anywhere from a few dollars daily to hundreds of dollars a night.

We have listed examples of accommodation in each regional section.

LOCAL TRANSPORT

Air

Thai Airways, the domestic airline, is first class. They have flights —
  Bangkok — Chiang Mai — at least 5 times a day (one hour).
  Bangkok — Phuket — at least 3 times a day (one hour).
  Bangkok — Surat Thani — at least twice a day (one hour).
  Bangkok — Hat Yai — at least 3 times a day (one hour fifteen minutes).

The reverse flights have the same frequency.

Air schedules may be checked by telephoning Thai Airways in Bangkok on 282 7649 or 282 7151, or Bangkok Airways on 523 7116.

Bangkok Airways operates 3 flights a day between Bangkok and Khorat.

Rail

An efficient rail system links major northern and north-eastern towns with the capital. A southern route permits the visitor to travel by train into Malaysia and Singapore. Domestic express trains comprise first, second and third-class carriages. Slower trains may have only third-class seats. Railway schedules can be obtained from Bangkok's Hualamphong Station, ph 223 7461.

Tickets for all classes may be purchased 90 days in advance at principal stations during the time advertised at each station, and at the Advance Booking Office in Bangkok Station, where the tickets to and from any station by all trains are obtainable on weekdays from 8.30am–6pm and weekends and official holidays from 8.30am–12 noon.

Validity of return tickets: all classes return on the same day for distance 1–100 km, 3 days for 101–200 km, 7 days for 201–500 km, 20 days for 501 km and over.

The following schedule, which should be used as a guide only, is for a single ticket, in bahts.

| *Northern Line* | | *Class of Travel* | | |
Bangkok to	*kms*	*1st*	*2nd*	*3rd*
Don Muang	22	18	10	5
Bang Pa-in	58	49	26	12
Ayutthaya	71	60	31	15
Lop Buri	133	111	57	28
Bah Takhii	193	157	80	39
Nakhon Sawan	246	197	99	48
Taphan Hin	319	245	122	58
Phichit	347	266	131	63
Phitsanulok	389	292	143	69
Uttaradit	485	356	172	82
Sila At	488	359	174	83
Den Chai	534	389	188	90
Mae Mo	609	440	211	100
Nakhon Lampang	642	463	221	106
Khun Tan	683	490	233	111
Lamphun	729	520	247	118
Chaing Mai	751	537	255	121
Muak Lek	152	126	65	31
Pak Chong	180	146	74	36
Nakhon Ratchasima	264	207	104	50
Surin	420	312	153	73
Sisaket	515	376	182	87
Ubon Ratchathani	575	416	200	95
Bua Yai	346	266	131	63
Ban Phai	408	306	150	71
Khon Kaen	450	333	162	77
Udon Thani	569	413	198	95
Nong Khai	624	450	215	103

Northern Line Bangkok to	kms	Class of Travel		
		1st	2nd	3rd
Hua Takhe	31			7
Chachoeng Sao	61			13
Prachin Buri	122			26
Kabin Buri	161			33
Aranyaprathet	255			48

Southern Line Bangkok to	kms	1st	2nd	3rd
Nakhon Pathom	64	54	28	14
Kanchanaburi	133	111	57	28
River Kwai Bridge	136	115	59	29
Nam Tok	210	168	85	41
Ratchaburi	117	99	52	25
Phetchaburi	167	138	71	34
Hua Hin	229	182	92	44
Prachuap Khiri Khan	318	245	122	58
Chumphon	485	356	172	82
Surat Thani	651	470	224	107
Thung Song	773	550	261	124
Trang	845	597	282	135
Nakhon Si Thammarat	832	590	279	133
Phatthalung	862	611	288	137
Hat Yai	945	664	313	149
Yala	1,055	738	346	165
Sungai Kolok	1,159	808	378	180
Padang Besar	990	694	326	156
Butterworth	1,149	927	431	222
Kuala Lumpur	1,531	1,432	659	361
Singapore	1,927	1,965	899	512

Supplementary Charges in bahts

Express train charge	30 per person
Rapid train charge	20 per person
Special express train charge	50 per person
Air-conditioned 2nd, 3rd coach charge	50 per person
Sleeping berth charges	
Air-conditioned 1st class berth — double	250 per person

Air-conditioned 2nd class berth	—	upper	170 per person
	—	lower	200 per person
2nd class berth	—	upper	70 per person
	—	lower	100 per person
2nd class berth (only special express)	—	upper	100 per person
	—	lower	150 per person
2nd class berth air-conditioned (only special express)	—	upper	200 per person
	—	lower	250 per person

Bus

A modern highway system reaches into all corners of the kingdom. Domestic bus services offer fast means of travel. Air-conditioned tour coaches offer more comfort.

Bangkok's Northern/North-eastern Bus Terminal is on Phahonyothin Road, ph 279 4484–7 (air) or 279 6222 (regular).

Bangkok's Southern Bus Terminal is on Charansanitwong Road, ph 411 4978–9 (air) and 411 0511 (regular).

Bangkok's Eastern Bus Terminal is on Sukhumwit Road, ph 391 3310 (air) and 392 2391 (regular).

The following schedules, which should be used as a guide only, are in bahts for a single ticket.

Air-conditioned Coaches to the North
(coaches leave from Northern Bus Terminal, Bangkok)

Destination	Fare	Departure Time
To Ban Mi	76 baht	5.55, 7.35, 9.20, 12.05, 14.10, 15.30, 17.30.
Chainat	763	9.00, 13.00, 17.00.
Chiang Mai	242	9.10, 9.30, 9.45, 10.00, 20.00, 20.30, 21.00, 21.10, 21.15, 21.30, 21.45.
Chiang Rai	283	19.30, 19.45, 19.50, 20.00.
Kamphaeng Petch	126	12.00, 22.30.

Destination	Fare	Departure Time
Lampang	207 baht	9.30, 11,00, 20.30, 21.30, 22.00.
Lamphun	227	20.20.
Lop Buri	60	5.00 and every 20 minutes to 20.30.
Lom Sak	137	8.30, 9.30, 10.30, 11.50, 13.00, 15.15, 16.00, 23.15, 23.30, 24.00.
Mae Sai	305	8.00, 19.00, 19.15, 19.30, 19.45, 19.55.
Mae Sot	179	22.15.
Nan	252	20.10, 20.20, 20.30.
Nakhon Sawan	87	7.00, 8.00, 12.00, 14.10, 15.00, 16.00, 18.00.
Phrae	213	20.30, 20.50.
Phayao	254	20.00.
Phitsanulok	171	7.00, 9.00, 10.45, 11.00, 11.10, 14.00, 16.00, 16.30, 22.00, 22.05, 22.30.
Phichit	125	11.50, 16.00, 22.10.
Sawankhalok	166	10.40.
Sing Buri	60	6.30, 8.30, 10.30, 11.30, 12.30, 13.30, 14.30, 15.40, 16.30, 18.00.
Sukhothai	153	10.40, 22.20, 22.40.
Suphan Buri	60	6.05, 7.05, 7.45, 8.25, 9.05, 9.45, 10.25, 11.05, 11.45, 12.25, 13.05, 13.45, 14.25, 15.05, 15.45, 16.25, 17.05, 17.45, 18.25, 19.05, 19.55, 21.05.
Tak	146	13.00, 22.10, 22.30.

Destination	Fare	Departure Time
Uthai Thani	92 baht	9.50, 16.45, 17.50.
Uttaradit	186	10.40, 11.00, 21.45, 22.00.

Air-conditioned Coaches to the South
(coaches leave from the Southern Bus Terminal, Bangkok)

Destination	Fare	Departure
Chumphon	160 baht	21.30, 21.40, 21.50, 22.00.
Hat Yai	339	17.30 and every 15 minutes to 20.15.
Hua Hin — Pran Buri	74–87	6.00 and every one hour to 20.00.
Kanchanaburi	53	6.00, 7.00, 8.00, 8.45, 9.30, 10.15, 11.00, 12.00, 12.45, 13.30, 14.15, 15.00, 15.45, 16.30, 17.18, 18.00, 20.99, 21.30.
Krabi	290	19.00, 20.00.
Nakhon Pathom	24	7.30 and every 30 minutes to 22.30.
Narathiwat	414	18.30.
Nakhon Si Thammarat	270	9.00, 18.30, 18.50, 19.10, 19.30, 19.50.
Pattani	382	18.00.
Phang Nga	294	19.30.
Phetburi	54	6.00, 7.30, 9.00, 10.30, 12.00, 13.30, 15.00, 16.30, 18.00, 9.30.
Prachuap Khiri Khan	105	8.00, 12.00, 16.30.
Phatthalung	297	20.00.
Phuket	299	19.00.

Destination	Fare	Departure Time
Ratchaburi	45 baht	7.00 and every hour to 12.00, 12.45, 3.30, 14.15, 15.00, 15.45, 16.40, 17.15, 8.00, 18.45, 19.30, 0.15, 21.00, 21.45, 2.30.
Ranong	198	9.30, 20.20, 20.40, 21.05, 21.10.
Samut Songkhram	33	6.30, 7.30 and every 30 minutes to 12.00, 13.00, 14.00, 15.00 and every 30 minutes to 20.30.
Samut Island	288	20.00.
Satun	355	18.30.
Surat Thani	225	20.20, 20.40.
Trang	314	19.50.
Yala	384	19.10.

Car

In order to hire a car, visitors must be in possession of a valid International Driving Licence. English-language road signs and maps are commonplace, and the Petroleum Authority of Thailand, Caltex, Esso and Shell maintain nationwide networks of petrol pumps and service stations. Premium grade gasoline is approximately 50 US cents per litre ($1.90 US gallon) in the Bangkok area. Marginally higher prices prevail in outlying provinces. Traffic drives on the left hand side of the road officially, but keep an eye out, the locals aren't the greatest drivers in the world.

Visitors should be warned that the majority of rental agencies for jeeps, motor scooters and motorbikes, do not carry insurance. Hire contracts with many operators make it clear the customer is liable for any damage to the vehicle, or for any injuries arising from an accident. Always check the contract before entering into any hire agreement.

One thing which can be a bit confusing to the newcomer is that the capital of each province has the same name as the province.

Once you know this it makes reading the road map, and touring guides, a little easier.

Taxi
Hotel limousines, with fixed rates, are the most convenient form of urban transportation. Fares on private taxis must be bargained beforehand.

FOOD
The Thai love of good food ensures excellent dining nationwide.

Thai cuisine is distinctive thanks to liberal use of spicy ingredients, and combines the best of Chinese and Indian culinary traditions — noodles, curries, sweet and sour dishes, slow-cooked and fast-cooked ingredients, exotic spices and condiments.

Thai dishes visitors can profitably enjoy include:

Kaeng Chut — mild vegetable broth with shrimp, chicken or pork.

Tom Yam Kung — shrimp soup seasoned with chillies, lemon grass and lime leaves.

Khao Thom Pla/Kung/Mu — rice soup flavoured with ginger, pepper and coriander, and containing fish or shrimps or pork.

Khao Man Kai — Plain rice flavoured with chicken dripping and topped with steamed chicken slices.

Khao Na Phet — plain rice topped by roast duck slices, ginger and wild cabbage.

Khao Na Mu — plain rice topped with sliced roast pork.

Khao Rat Na Nua — plain rice with beef slices, vegetables fried in oyster sauce and beef gravy.

Khao Phat Mu/Kai/Kung/Pu — fried rice with pork or chicken, or shrimps or crab.

Kuai Tiao Rat Na — rice noodles topped with kale and gravy and either pork or chicken.

Kuai Tiao Nam — rice noodle soup with fish balls, beansprouts, dried shrimps and pork.

Khai Yat Sai — omelette stuffed with peas, onions and minced pork.

Yam Nua/Pla Muk — spicy salad with beef or squid.

Kaeng Masaman — Muslim-style sweet beef curry.

Po Pia — spring rolls stuffed with minced pork, crab and cooked beansprouts.

Kai Phat Phrik — chicken fried with chillies and onions.

Kai Yang — Thai-style barbecued chicken.

Visitors can easily find other appetising food. Chinese food in Thailand, normally quite bland, is second to none. Major European, Levantine, Asian and Oriental cuisines are represented in gourmet restaurants. American, English and Continental breakfasts are served in most hotels, and numerous ubiquitous coffeeshops specialise in European dishes. Western-style fast food shops, snack bars and ice cream parlours are becoming popular with Thais.

Thai fruits, including mangoes, mangosteens, durians, pineapples, watermelons, papayas, rambutans, longang, linchees, tamarinds, pomegranates, palm fruits, oranges, pomeloes, jackfruits and more than 20 kinds of bananas, are in a class of their own. Also, many visitors leave convinced Thai seafood is incomparable.

Bottled water is served in most restaurants.

ENTERTAINMENT

Nationwide, nightclubs, gourmet restaurants, discotheques, concert halls, teahouses, cocktail lounges, amusement parks, bars, theatres, art galleries and cinemas lure pleasure seekers throughout the year. Plus it has its fair share of massage parlours.

Thailand's English-language newspapers carry daily listings of concerts, exhibitions, displays and cinema programmes. Complimentary weekly tourist publications such as "Where", "Bangkok This Week", "Pattaya This Week" etc., contain additional information with emphasis on dining and nightlife attractions.

SHOPPING

Thailand offers some of the world's best shopping. Bargains are found in bazaars, air-conditioned shopping centres, boutiques, "hole-in-the-wall" shops, multi-storied department stores and government-approved emporiums.

Gifts and souvenirs can be — Thai silks, cottons, nielloware, silverware, bronzeware, pottery and celadon, antiques, umbrellas, rattan and wickerwork, dolls, paintings, lacquerware, pewterware, precious stones and finished jewellery, plus a dazzling range of folk handicrafts. International standard ready-made sports and leisurewear is inexpensive; and quality tailors and dressmakers offer reliable 24-hour services in Bangkok and major tourism destinations.

Anyone who has been shopping in Hong Kong and been horrified at the brassy yellow colour of the gold chains, etc. will be delighted with the soft, 'real gold' look of Thailand's jewellery. The prices are more reasonable as well.

If you are looking for a special souvenir of Thailand, we suggest that you shop around for a reasonably-priced jade Thai Buddha. To non-believers, the Thai Buddha seems so much more elegant than the fat, jovial-looking gentleman found in other parts of South-East Asia. When you do find the right one, make sure it is packed well, as the tip of his hat is fragile and could easily be broken if you have to put it in your suitcase.

Shoppers can take advantage of a bi-monthly pocket-sized Shopping Guide published by the Tourism Authority of Thailand (TAT). The complimentary publication contains useful shopping tips, maps of major shopping areas, and a comprehensive list of TAT-listed shops in Bangkok, Pattaya, Chiang Mai and Phuket.

The Tourist Authority of Thailand issues an Emblem of Standard to souvenir shops and restaurants which have been screened by the Sub-Committee to Promote Souvenir Shops Standard, and the Sub-Committee to Promote Restaurant and Foodshop Standard, certifying to their standard and services. This emblem is displayed in the windows of the various establishments, and visitors are advised to patronise these, as you will be sure of not being 'ripped off', always a worry when buying, and dining, in a foreign country.

SIGHTSEEING
The sightseeing attractions are listed in each section. We also include an itinerary for each area, as suggested by the Tourism Authority of Thailand.

THAI SPORTS AND GAMES
Golf, soccer, boxing, badminton, tennis, bowling and snooker

figure prominently among international sports enjoyed by Thais. Indigenous games and sports include world-famous Thai 'kick' boxing, takrao, kite-fighting and boat racing.

Thai boxing developed as a form of self-defence during the Ayutthaya period (1350–1767). Boxers are forbidden to bite, spit or wrestle. However, they may kick, shove and push, and unrestrainedly use bare feet, legs, elbows and shoulders, besides fists, to batter each other into submission. Modern boxers wear conventional boxing gloves instead of yesteryear's hemp bandages embedded with ground glass.

Thai boxing is featured every day at Bangkok's Ratchadamnoen and Lumphini Stadiums (Mon, Wed, Thurs and Sun at Ratchadamnoen, and Tue, Fri and Sat at Lumphini).

Traditionally, takrao is played by a loosely formed circle of men who use their feet, knees, thighs, chests and shoulders to pass a woven rattan ball to each other, endeavouring to keep it off the ground, and eventually kick it into a basket suspended above their heads.

Kites have been popular in Thailand since at least the 1240s and have been profitably used in warfare. In 1690, an Ayutthaya governor quelled a north-eastern city-state's rebellion by flying massive kites over the besieged city and bombing it into submission with jars of explosives.

Today, kite flying is either an individual pleasure or a competitive sport. During summer months opposing teams fly male (Chula) and female (Pakpao) kites in a surrogate battle of the sexes. The small, agile Pakpao tries to fell the more cumbersome Chula while the male kite tries to ensnarl the female kite and drag it back into male territory.

Boat racing is featured at many country fairs which celebrate the end of the annual Buddhist Rains Retreat. The long, narrow, low-slung wooden boats are festooned with flags and flowers, manned by oarsmen and raced with great gusto. The most noteworthy boat races are in Nan, east of Chiang Mai, the south's Surat Thani, the north-east's Nakhon Phanom and Pathumthani near Bangkok.

BANGKOK

Bangkok, City of Angels, is the Orient's most cosmopolitan city. Created the Thai capital in 1782 by the first monarch of the present Chakri dynasty, Bangkok is a national treasure house and Thailand's spiritual, cultural, political, commercial, educational and diplomatic centre. Approximately one in every ten Thais is a Bangkokian.

Major attractions include glittering Buddhist temples, palaces, floating markets, timeless 'Venice of the East' canal scenes, an almost legendary nightlife, and numerous shopping centres.

HOW TO GET THERE

Bangkok's Don Muang is Thailand's major international airport, and most visitors arrive here on international flights.

The airport is 25 km (16 miles) north of the city and there is a regular airport bus service to the City Terminal (Asia Hotel) every thirty minutes from 6am–11pm.

On arrival at the airport, it is best to go straight to the Tourism Authority of Thailand desk, for information on how to get into the city. Do not be persuaded from this by the many people offering you the use of their taxis, or you will be in great danger of being 'ripped off'.

TOURIST INFORMATION

The Head Office of the Tourism Authority of Thailand is on Ratchadamnoen Nok Avenue, ph 282 1143–7, and is open seven days a week, including public holidays.

Several complimentary tourism publications are also available at hotels, airline offices and major retail outlets' counters.

ACCOMMODATION

There is no shortage of accommodation in Bangkok, and here we have listed a rather wide selection. The prices given are in baht for a double room per night, and should be used as a guide only. They

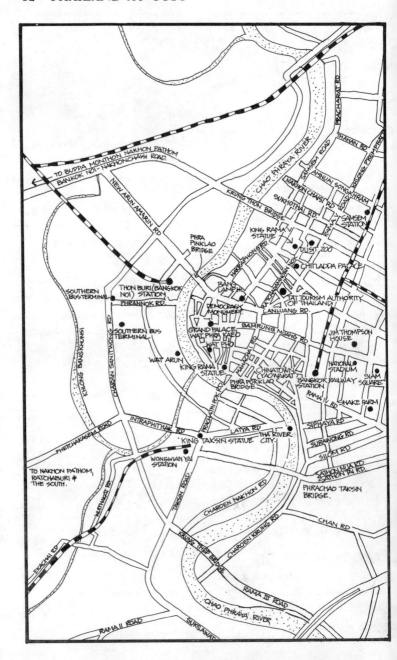

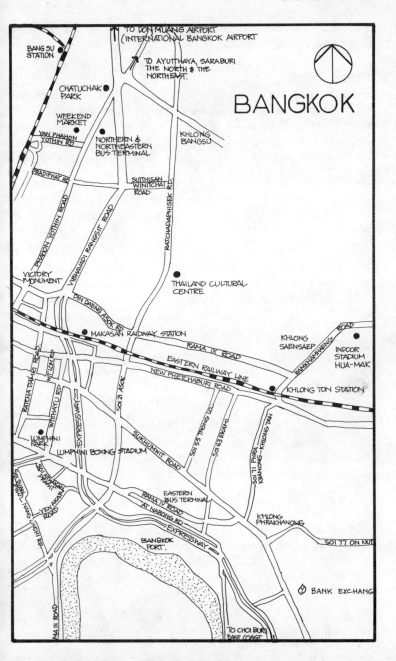

are subject to a 10% service charge and 11% government tax. The telephone area code is 02.

Deluxe Hotels

Central Plaza, 1695 Phahonyothin Road, ph 541 1234. Situated approximately halfway between the airport and the city centre, the hotel has 607 guest rooms. Facilities include several restaurants, lounge bar and disco, swimming pool, sauna and fitness centre. The Central Department store is next door — 3,000–3,400 baht.

Dusit Thani, 946 Rama IV Road, ph 236 0450. Set in beautiful grounds in the centre of the city, the hotel has 525 guest rooms. Facilities include 7 restaurants, supper club, disco, swimming pool, health club, sauna, spa, squash and tennis — 3,125–4,750 baht.

Hilton International, 2 Wireless Road, Bangkok, ph 253 0123. With 343 guest rooms, the hotel's facilities include restaurants. coffee shop, cocktail lounge, health club, tennis court, gymnasium, swimming pool, videotheque and shopping arcade — 3,200–3,600 baht.

The Landmark, 138 Sukhumvit Road, ph 254 0404. There are 415 guest rooms with computer keyboard for sending faxes and telexes. Facilities include 4 restaurants, 24-hour coffee shop, nightclub, pub, health club, outdoor swimming pool, squash court, shopping arcade and jacuzzi — 3,200–3,400.

Montien Hotel, 54 Surawongse Road, ph 234 8060. Recently refurbished, the hotel has 485 guest rooms and 35 suites. Facilities include 24-hour coffee shop, Chinese restaurant, brasseries, piano bar and cocktail lounge, theatre, swimming pool and shopping arcade — 2,200–3,500 baht.

The Oriental, 48 Oriental Avenue, ph 236 0400. With 394 guest rooms, the Oriental is not only the best hotel in Thailand, it is one of the best in the world. It has every facility anyone could want, and doubles cost 4,100–5,500 baht. (Suites go as high as 36,000 baht.)

Regent of Bangkok, 155 Ratchadamri Road, ph 251 6127. Located opposite the Royal Bangkok Sports Club, the hotel has 400 guest rooms, and facilities include restaurant, bar/cocktail lounge, coffee shop, health club, shopping arcade, and the largest hotel swimming pool in Bangkok — 3,000–3,800 baht.

Royal Orchid Sheraton, 2 Captain Bush Lane, Shiphaya Road, ph 234 5599. Situated on the banks of the Chao Phraya River, the hotel has 775 guest rooms, all with river views. Facilities include 4 restaurants, 2 bars, balcony lounge, nightclub, swimming pool, health club, tennis court and shopping complex — 2,800–3,200 baht.

Shangri-La, 89 Soi Wat Suan Plu, New Road, Bangrak, ph 236 777. Set on the banks of the Chao Phraya River, the hotel has 650 guest rooms and 47 suites, all with river views. Facilities include 4 restaurants, coffee shop, barbeque terrace, health club, swimming pool, and tennis and squash courts — 4,500–5,400 baht.

Siam Inter Continental, 967 Rama I Road, Pratumwan, ph 253 0355. Has 400 guest rooms and facilities include restaurant, coffee shop, health club, tennis court, swimming pool, golf course, night club and shopping arcade — 3,000–3,400 baht.

Superior Hotels

Airport Hotel, 333 Choet Wudhakat Road, ph 566 1020. Opposite the airport, the hotel has 300 guest rooms, restaurants, bars, coffee shop, health club, swimming pool and night club — 2,904 baht (includes service fee and tax).

Asia Hotel, 296 Phayathai Road, ph 215 0808. The hotel is situated near Rajathevi Junction, minutes from the business and entertainment centres, and has recently been renovated. There are 650 guest rooms, and facilities include 6 restaurants, coffee shop, cocktail lounge and bar, cabaret, 2 swimming pools, health club and gym — 2,420 baht.

Bangkok Palace, 1091/336 New Phetburi Road, ph 253 0500. There are 690 guest rooms, and facilities include restaurants, bars, coffee shop, health club, snooker club, swimming pool, night club and shopping arcade — 2,200–2,600 baht.

The Imperial, Wireless Road, Patumwan, ph 254 0111. Facilities include restaurants, cocktail lounge, health club, swimming pool, gymnasium, shopping arcade — 2,730 baht.

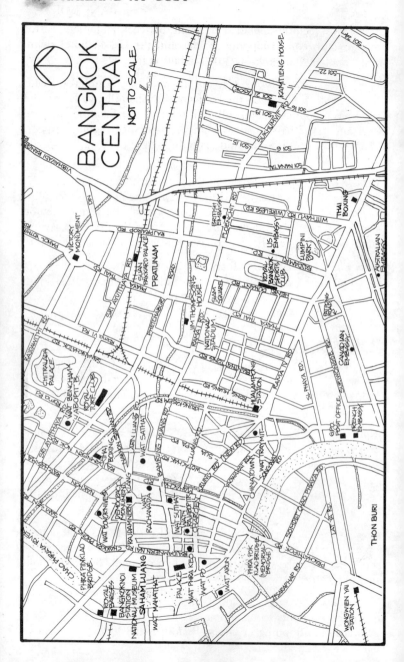

Indra Regent Hotel, Rajprarob, Pratunam, ph 252 1111. Located close to the department stores and sidewalk markets, the hotel has 450 guest rooms. Facilities include several restaurants, coffee shop, swimming pool, health club and the Den Disco — 2,300–2,500 baht.

Mandarin, 662 Rama IV Road, ph 233 4980. Close to the main shopping and entertainment centres, and has 343 guest rooms. Facilities include grill room, 24-hour coffee lounge, swimming pool, cocktail lounge and night club — 1,920–2,300 baht.

Manohra, 412 Surawongse Road, ph 234 5070. A comfortable hotel with 240 guest rooms not far from Chao Phraya River and Silom Road area. Facilities include restaurant, coffee shop, cocktail lounge, nightclub, swimming pool and shopping arcade — 1,694 baht.

Narai, 222 Silom Road, ph 233 3350. Situated in the heart of the major shopping district, the hotel has 500 rooms, including 36 suites, and has been recently renovated. Facilities include rooftop revolving restaurant (the only one in Bangkok), 2 other restaurants, coffee shop, cocktail lounge, 2 bars, health club, swimming pool and shopping arcade — 2,100 baht.

Princess, 269 Larn Luang Road, ph 281 3088. Hotel has 170 guest rooms and facilities include restaurants, coffee shop, swimming pool and shopping arcade — 2,700 baht.

Royal River, 670/805 Charansanitwong Road, ph 433 0300. Opened in 1987, the hotel is on the Chao Phraya River, and has 404 guest rooms, most with river views. Facilities include health club, sauna, spa, swimming pool, disco, two restaurants, coffee shop, cocktail lounge, and shuttle service across the river to the River City shopping area — 2,200–2,400 baht.

Standard Hotels

Bangkok Centre, 328 Rama IV Road, ph 235 1780 — 225 guest rooms — restaurant, nightclub and shopping arcade — 1,332 baht.

Continental, 971/16 Phahonyothin Road, ph 278 1385 — 122 guest rooms — restaurant, bar, coffee shop and night club — 650 baht.

Florida, 43 Phayathai Road, ph 245 3221 — 107 guest rooms — restaurant, coffee shop and swimming pool — 600 baht.

Golden Dragon, 20/21 Ngarm Wongwan Road, ph 589 5141 — 120 guest rooms — restaurant, bar, coffee shop, swimming pool and shopping arcade — 711 baht (including service fee and tax).

Grace, 12 Nana North, Sukhumvit Soi 3, ph 253 0651 — 542 guest rooms — restaurant, bar, coffee shop, health club, swimming pool, night club and shopping arcade — 678–823 baht.

Manhattan, 13 Sukhumvit Road, Soi 15, ph 252 7141 — 200 rooms guest rooms — restaurant, bar, coffee shop, swimming pool and night club — 1,200 baht.

Nana, 4 Soi Nana Tai, Sikhumvit Road, ph 252 0121 — 325 guest rooms — restaurant, bar, coffee shop, swimming pool, video-theque, disco and shopping arcade — 650–750 baht.

New Fuji, 299-301 Surawongse Road, ph 234 5364 — 66 guest rooms — restaurant, bar, swimming pool, night club and shopping arcade — 888–999 baht.

New Peninsula, 295/3 Surawongse Road, ph 234 3910 — 113 guest rooms — restaurant, bar, coffee shop, swimming pool, video-theque and shopping arcade — 944–1,166 baht (including service fee and tax).

New Trocadero, 343 Surawongse Road, ph 234 8920 — 131 guest rooms — restaurant, bar, coffee shop, swimming pool, snooker club, night club and shopping arcade — 833–1,110 baht.

Ra-Jah, 18 Soi 4 Sukhumvit Road, ph 251 8563 — 450 guest rooms — restaurant, bar, swimming pool and shopping arcade — 992 baht.

Rose, 118 Surawongse Road, ph 233 7695 — 105 guest rooms — restaurant, bar, coffee shop and videotheque — 680 baht.

Victory, 322 Silom, ph 233 9060 — 122 guest rooms — coffee shop, videotheque and shopping arcade — 820 baht.

Viengtai, 42 Tanee Road, Banglumpoo, ph 282 8119 — 217 guest rooms — coffee shop, swimming pool and shopping arcade — 678 baht.

Windsor, Soi 20 Sukhumvit Road, ph 258 0160 — 250 guest rooms — restaurant, bar, coffee shop, swimming pool, disco and shopping arcade — 1,800–2,500 baht.

YMCA (Collins House), 27 Sathon Tai Road, ph 287 2727 — 147 guest rooms — coffee shop and swimming pool — 1,000 baht.

Budget Hotels

Federal, 27 Sukhumvit Road, Soi 11, ph 253 0175 — 93 guest rooms — restaurant, coffee shop and swimming pool — 540 baht.

Fortuna, 19 Sukhumvit Road, Soi 5, ph 251 5121 — 110 guest rooms — restaurant, coffee shop, swimming pool and disco — 600 baht.

Liberty, 215 Pradipat Road, ph 271 0880 — 196 guest rooms — coffee shop and swimming pool — 460–700 baht.

Malaysia, 53 Soi Ngamdupli, Rama IV Road, ph 286 3582 — 120 guest rooms — restaurant, bar and swimming pool — 396–500 baht.

Miramar, 777 Minsen Corner, Samyod, ph 222 4191 — 150 guest rooms — restaurant, coffee shop and shopping arcade — 685 baht.

Parliament, 402 Visuthikasat Road, ph 281 7237 — 92 guest rooms — restaurant — 480 baht.

Prince, 269 Larn Luang Road, ph 281 3088 — 200 guest rooms — bar, coffee shop, swimming pool, videotheque and shopping arcade — 484–880 baht.

Ramada, 1169 New Road, ph 234 8971 — 62 guest rooms — bar and coffee shop — 480 baht.

Royal Plaza, 30 Nares Road, Bangrak, ph 234 3789 — 245 guest rooms — restaurant, bar, coffee shop and shopping arcade — 650–800 baht.

Siam, 1777 New Phetburi Road, ph 252 5081 — 120 guest rooms — restaurant, bar, swimming pool and shopping arcade — 690 baht.

Thai, 78 Prachatiphatai Road, ph 282 2831 — 100 guest rooms — restaurant, bar, swimming pool, videotheque and shopping arcade — 620 baht.

Guest Houses

These are an inexpensive alternative to staying in a hotel, and are becoming more popular with tourists who are willing to go without a lot of life's little luxuries.

Amarin Guest House, 593-595 Chakraphet Road, ph 222 0532 — 16 rooms with fans — 120–200 baht.

Apple Guest House, 49/5 Chao Fah Road, Chanasongkharm, ph 281 6838 — 20 rooms (no fans) — 80 baht.

Bangkok Youth Hostel, 25/2 Phitsanulok Road, ph 282 0950 — 20 rooms (no fans) — 150 baht.

Chart Guest House, 61 Khao-San Road, Banglampoo, ph 281 0803 — 55 single rooms with fans — 50–100 baht per person.

✗*James Guest House*, 116/1 Prachatiphatai Road, ph 280 0362 — 30 rooms with fans — 80 baht.

KT Guest House, 14 Suthisarn Road, ph 277 4035 — 20 rooms with fans, a restaurant and coffee shop — 250 baht.

Lee Guest House, 21/38-39 Soi Ngamdupli, Rama IV Road, ph 286 2069 — 24 rooms with fans — 100 baht.

Lek Guest House, 125 Khao San Road, ph 282 6223 — 20 rooms with fans — 80–100 baht.

New Siam Guest House, 21 Soi Chanasongkhram, Phra Athit Road, ph 282 4554 — 20 rooms with fans — 100 baht.

Peachy Guest House, 10 Phra Athit Road, ph 281 6471 — 250 baht.

Prasuri Guest House, 85/1 Soi Prasuri, Dinsor Road, ph 280 1428 — 21 rooms with fans — 140 baht.

P. Guest House, 151-157 Trok Sa-Ke, Ranao Road, ph 224 1967 — 18 rooms (no fans) — 100 baht.

Safty Guest House, 1036/6 Rama IV Road, Yannawa, ph 286 8904 — 17 rooms with fans — 80 baht.

Sri Guest House, 1 Soi 38 Sukhumvit Road, ph 381 1309 — 33 air-conditioned rooms and coffee shop and tennis court — 500 baht.

SV Guest House, 19/35-36 Sukhumvit Road, Soi 19, ph 253 1747 — 20 air-conditioned rooms — 300 baht.

TT Guest House, 138 Soi Wat Mahaphutharam, Si Phraya, ph 236 3053 — 30 rooms with fans — 120 baht.

LOCAL TRANSPORT

Bus
Government-operated regular buses, airconditioned buses and mini-buses are economical (2 baht fares on regular buses, 15 baht on air-conditioned buses) but lack English language destination boards.

Taxi
Hotel taxis have fixed rates. Taxis cruising the streets of Bangkok rarely use their meters, so fares must be agreed upon before boarding.

Car
The Yellow Pages of the Bangkok telephone directory list local and international car rental companies. Visitors are advised to 'shop around' since there is big difference in rates and conditions between the different companies.

NOTE: The main streets of Bangkok are intersected by smaller streets, sometimes cul-de-sacs, which are called 'sois'. If one of these smaller streets does not have a name, it has a number, and those on one side of the main street are odd numbers, and on the other they are even. This tends to be a bit confusing when you first arrive, but once you get used to it, the system works fine.

EATING OUT

There is no shortage of restaurants, beer cellars, pubs, coffee shops and fast food outlets offering a choice of every type of food imaginable. Indeed, all major European, Levantine, Asian and Oriental cuisines are represented in gourmet restaurants which may be air-conditioned, opulent and expensive, or simple open-air establishments where the accent is exclusively on excellent, reasonably priced food.

Leading hotels regularly stage foreign food festivals and buffets featuring local and foreign dishes, including some of the world's finest seafood.

Thai Restaurants with Thai classical dance
Baan Thai, 7 Sukhumvit Soi 32, ph 258 5403 — nightly 7–10pm; Kodak Show, Pool Side, Oriental Hotel, New Road, ph 236 0040 — Thurs & Sat 11am–12 noon; Maneeya's Lotus Room, Phloenchit Road, ph 252 6312 — nightly 7–10pm; Nopakao Room, Chao Phya Restaurant, Pin Klao Bridge, Arun Amarin Road, ph 242 2389 — nightly 8–9.30pm; Piman, 46 Sukhumvit Soi 49, ph 258 7866 — nightly 8–10pm; Ruen Thep, Silom Village Trade Centre, ph 233 9447 — nightly 7.30–10pm; Sala Norasing, Sukhumvit Soi 4 (Nana Tai), ph 251 5797 — nightly 7.30–10pm; Sala Thai, Indra Regent Hotel, Ratchaprarop Road, ph 251 1111 — Mon–Sat, 7.30–9.30pm; Sala Rim Naam, Charoen Nakhon Road (opposite Oriental Hotel), ph 437 6221 — nightly 7.30–10pm; Sukhothai, Dusit Thani Hotel, Rama IV Road, ph 233 1130 — nightly 7.30–10pm; Suwanahong, Si Ayutthaya Road, ph 245 4448 — nightly 7.30–10pm; Tump-Nak-Thai, 546/2 Ratchadaphisek Road, ph 276 1810 — nightly 8–9.30pm.

Thai Restaurants
Bankaeo Ruenkwan, 212 Sukhumvit Soi 12, ph 251 8229; Bussaracum, 35 Soi Pipat 2 (off Convent Road), ph 235 8915; Datchanee, 18/2–4 Prachathipatai Road, ph 281 9332; D'Jit Pochana, 62 Sukhumvit Soi 20, ph 391 6401, and 1082 Phahonyothin Road, ph 279 5000; Khanom Buang Sukhothai, Sukhothai Soi 4, ph 281 3496; Khun Ying, 55 Sukhumvit Soi 63, ph 391 5769; Kruathai, 54 Ngamdupli Road (Malaysia Hotel), ph 286 3582; Samae San, 65 Suykhumvit Soi 31, ph 258 4582; Ton Tum Rub, 15–17 Sukhumvit Soi 8, ph 253 5154; Ton Khroeng, 299 Soi Thong Lor, Sukhumvit, ph 391 8703; Wang Kaeo, 74–74/1 Ratchadaphisek Road, ph 245 9134.

Thai and Chinese Restaurants
Bangkok Maxim, 62/3–4 Ratchadamri Road, ph 252 6310; Chan-
phen Restaurant, 1031/1 Rama IV Road, ph 286 0933; Chao Phya
Restaurant, Pin Klao Bridge, Arun Amarin Road, ph 424 2389;
Chiu Chau, Ambassador Hotel, Sukhumvit Road, ph 251 5141;
Coca, 416 Henri Dunant Road, 251 6337; Downtown, 20 Soi
Chidlom, ph 252 1859, and 430/6–10 Siam Square, ph 252 0237;
Dynasty, Hyatt Central Plaza Hotel, 1691 Phahonyothin Road,
ph 541 1048; Fu Lu Su, 23 Ratchaprasong Road, ph 252 6526;
Golden Dragon, 108–114 Sukhumvit Road, ph 251 4553; Grand
Shangarila Restaurant, 58/4 Thaniya Road, ph 234 2045; Hoi
Thien Lao, 308 Sua Pa Road, ph 221 2685; Honey Restaurant, 424
Surawong Road, ph 234 9968; Jade Garden, Montien Hotel, 54
Surawong Road, ph 234 8060; Maria, Ratchadamnoen Klang
Avenue, ph 221 5211; Mary, 414/5–7 Henri Dunant Road, ph 251
6802; Ming Palace, Indra Regent Hotel, Ratchaprarob Road,
ph 251 1111; New Rincome, 144 Silom Road, ph 235 2781; Rose
La Moon, 154/5–6 Sukhumvit Soi 21, ph 391 7351; Ruen Phae,
622/103 Charansanitwong Road, ph 424 7563; Si Fa, 434 Siam
Square, ph 251 5517, and 47/19–22 Ratchadamri Road, ph 253
7806, and 942/31 Rama IV Road, ph 235 3290; Si Thaiderm, 192
Lumpini Park, ph 252 6330; Silom Village, Silom Road, ph 233
9447; Sorn Daeng, 78 Ratchadamnoen Klang Avenue, ph 224
3088; Tien Kong Restaurant, 77 Soi Nana Nua, Sukhumvit Road,
ph 251 4881; Vijit Restaurant, 77/2 Ratchadamnoen Klang
Avenue, ph 281 6472; Tab Kaeo, Ratchadaphisek Road, ph 246
2380; Khum Luang, Ratchadaphisek Road, ph 246 3272; Ban
Bung, 32/10 Ratchadaphisek Road, ph 277 7563; Bua Tong,
Ratchadaphisek Road, ph 245 5545; Chao Khun, 68 Ratchadaphisek Road, ph 246 2145; Na Thong, Ratchadaphisek Road,
ph 246 2160; Wang Kaeo, 74–74/1 Ratchadaphisek Road, ph 245
6431; Tam Nak Thai, Ratchadaphisek Road, ph 277 8833; Ya
Kha, 87 Lad Phrao Soi 112, ph 514 0005.

American Restaurants
Beefeater Steak House, 9/4–5 Thaniya Road, ph 234 3590;
Bobby's Arms, 114/1–2 Soi Charuwan, Silom Road, ph 233 6828;
Orlando, Florida Hotel, 43 Phayathai Road, ph 245 3221–4.

Arabic and Muslim Restaurants
Akbar, Sukhumvit Soi 3, ph 242 5582; Aladdin, 4/6 Sukhumvit Soi 3, Nana Nua; Alibaba, 391/3–4 Silom Road, ph 234 6982; Dean, 545/3 Silom Road, ph 234 8407; Muslim Restaurant, 1217–9 New Road, ph 233 1010; Sabu Muslim Restaurant, 17–19 Pramuan Road, ph 233 3047.

French Restaurants
Bon Vivant Grill, Tawana, Sheraton Hotel, 80 Surawongse Road, ph 233 5160; Le Gourmet, Montien Hotel, 54 Surawongse Road, ph 234 8060; Le Metropolitain, 135/6 Gaysorn Road, ph 252 8364; Le Petit Moulin, 2/33 Sukhumvit Soi 22, ph 258 2852; Le Vendome, 153/1 Soi Mahatlek, Ratchadamri Road, ph 252 6753; La Cave, Erawan Hotel, 494 Ratchadamri Road, ph 252 9100; La Palomo, 26 Mahaesak Road, ph 233 3853.

German Restaurants
Bierstrube, 569 Sukhumvit Road (between Soi 31 and 33), ph 258 9303; Haus Muenchen, 4 Sukhumvit Soi 15, ph 252 5776; Singha Bier Haus, 179 Soi Asoke, Sukhumvit Road, ph 258 3951; Hungarian Restaurant, Nick's No. 1, 1 Sathon Tai Road, ph 286 2258.

Indian Restaurants
Cafe India, 460/8 Surawongse Road (opposite Trocadero Hotel), ph 234 1720; Galaxy Restaurant and Night Club, 19 Rama IV Road, ph 235 5000; Moti Mahal Restaurant and Bar, 18–20 Old Chartered Bank Lane, New Road, ph 233 5621; Omar Khayyam, Sukhumvit Soi 3, ph 253 3380; Sheeh Mahal Restaurant, 1/22 Soi 3 Nana Nua (near Grace Hotel), ph 250 0203.

Indonesian Restaurant
Indonesia, 1975 New Phetchburi Road, ph 314 4170.

Italian Restaurants
Giorgio's Restaurant, The Royal Orchid Sheraton Hotel, ph 224 2083; Hotte Shop, Soi Lang Suan, Phloenchit Road, ph 251 8007; Italian Pavilion, 19 Sukhumvit Soi 4, ph 252 4257; Libra Restaurant, 36 Sukhumvit Soi 18, ph 391 1113; The Shack, 901

Sukhumvit Soi 49, ph 258 7962; Trattoria Da Roberto, Plaza Arcade, Patpong 2, ph 233 6851.

Japanese Restaurants
Akamon, 233 Soi Asoke, Sukhumvit Road, ph 258 3886; Aoyama, Rama IV Road, ph 233 4832; Asuka, 23/11 Silom Road, ph 233 9697; Daikoku, 960 Rama IV Road, ph 233 1495; Hanaya, 683 Si Phya Road, ph 233 3080; Kikusiu, 133 Pan St. Silom Road, ph 234 4031; Kyoto Restaurant, 9 Sukhumvit Soi 11, ph 252 8458; Kobe Steak House, 460 Soi Siam Square, Rama I Road, ph 251 1336; Mizu's Kitchen, 32 Patpong Road, ph 233 6447; Scochiku Restaurant, 62/9–10 Soi Taniya, Silom Road, ph 233 9694; Toukugawa Restaurant, Ambassador Hotel, ph 251 5141.

Korean Restaurants
Arirang, 106 Silom Road, ph 234 7869; First Korean Restaurant, 543 Silom Road, 234 2636; Korea House Restaurant, 448–50 Siam Square, ph 242 9398; New Korea Restaurant, 41/1 Sukhumvit Soi 19, ph 251 5273; Seoul Restaurant, 47 Ratchaprasong Shopping Centre, ph 252 9285; Uotake Restaurant, 41–43 Ratchaprasong Road, ph 251 1533.

Scandinavian Restaurants
Mermaid's Inn, 447 Sathon Tai Road, ph 233 0520; Mermaid's Rest, 6/1 Sukhumvit Soi 8 (Soi Preeda), ph 252 6648; Swiss Inn, 410/7–8 Soi 6 Siam Square, ph 251 0155; The Two Vikings Restaurant, 2 Soi 35 (Charoen Nivet), Sukhumvit Road, ph 258 8843.

Western Food Restaurants
Amigo's, Ambassador Hotel, ph 251 5141; Castillion Garden, Dusit Thani Hotel, ph 233 1130; Charly's International, 66 Sathon Nua Road, ph 234 9035; Fireplace Grill, President Hotel, ph 253 7557; Indra Grill, Indra Hotel, ph 251 1111; Le Normandie Grill, Oriental Hotel, ph 236 0040; Mario's Pizza, 135/18 Gaysorn Road, ph 251 6427; Neil's Tavern, 58/4 Soi Ruam Rudi, ph 251 5644; Rajah Hotel 24 Hours Coffee Shop and Siriporn Hall, 18 Soi 4 Sukhumvit Road, ph 252 5102; Siam Grill, Siam Inter-Continental Hotel, ph 253 0355; The Captain Bush Grill, Royal Orchid Sheraton Hotel, ph 224 2083; The Cup, Oriental Plaza, New Road, ph 234 1320; The Golden Poppy and The Greenery Coffee

Shop, The Rama Gardens Hotel, ph 579 5400; Your Place, 146 Soi
Thonglor, Sukhumvit, ph 391 4425; Zeppelin Airport Hotel, 333
Chert Wudhtakas Road, Don Muang, ph 523 9177.

Vegetarian Restaurants
Cafeteria Bangkok, Adventist Hospital, 430 Phitsanulok Road,
ph 281 1026; Himali Cha Cha, 1229/11 New Road, ph 235 1569;
Prakhai, 299–301 New Fuji Hotel, ph 234 5364; Whole Earth
Cafe, 93/3 Soi Lang Suan, Phloenchit Road, ph 252 5574.

ENTERTAINMENT
As the saying goes "one night in Bangkok and the world's your
oyster". Bangkok nightlife is legendary, and despite efforts by
officials to 'clean up' the city, prostitution is alive and well.

Thai massage is an old, respected art, but all the massage
parlours, of which there are hundreds, are not necessarily masters
of this art. If you would like to experience a true massage, it is best
to check with your hotel information desk as to the best place to
go, otherwise you could find yourself in an embarrassing situation.

Your hotel will also be able to provide you with a free booklet
entitled "Bangkok after Dark", which has information on all the
night spots, bars, discotheques, etc.

SHOPPING
Few cities can equal Bangkok's shopping opportunities, and most
of them are within walking distance of the major hotels.

One major shopping district is along Silom and Suriwong Roads,
close to the *Dusit Thani*, *Montien* and *Tawana Sheraton Hotels*. Here
there are Robinson's Department Store, the Charn Issara Shopping Centre, dozens of silk and antique shops, boutiques and
leather outlets.

Within walking distance of the Ratchaprasong Intersection
(Ploenchit, Rajdamri and Rama I Roads) are the Amarin Plaza
Shopping Centre and Central Department Store, the Ratchadamri
Arcade and Daimaru Department Store, and the Peninsula Arcade
and Galleries Lafayette. Many other department stores are found
on Ploenchit and Phetchaburi Roads.

Outside of these districts there are the Oriental Plaza, near the
Oriental Hotel; the River City Shopping Complex, near the *Royal
Orchid Sheraton Hotel*; the Siam Centre, near the *Siam Inter-
continental Hotel*; the Mah Boon Krong; and the Tokyu Depart-

ment Store, which is very popular with the younger generation.

Then there are the markets, which apart from offering the good bargain or two, have a colourful atmosphere, and allow you to try your bargaining skills. Pratunam, near the *Indra Hotel*, has mostly ready-made clothing, whereas the Phahurat Cloth Market, at the corner of Phahurat and Chakraphet Roads has well-priced fabrics. In Chinatown, Sampheng Lane and Yaowarat Road markets have countless shops selling gold, jewellery and other goods.

The biggest market, and definitely the most fascinating, is the Chatuchak Weekend Market, held in Chatuchak Park, near the *Central Plaza Hotel*. For sale here is everything that is made or grown in Thailand, and the market operates from 7am–6pm both days.

For duty-free goods, there are shops in the renovated Don Muang Airport, or the TAT Duty Free Shop at 888 Ploenchit Road, ph 253 6451. The latter is a real shopping experience, with over 2,900 square metres of shopping space decorated in traditional Thai style. The staff are multi-lingual and extremely courteous, and the range of goods for sale is astounding.

SIGHTSEEING

If you intend to see Bangkok on foot, buy a street map, and learn to count in Thai. There are few street signs in English. Also keep an eye on your bag and camera, as there are pickpockets around.

Inner Bangkok
Bordered by the Maenam Chao Phraya (River of Kings) and the Krung Kasem canal, this is an island containing most of the city's historic temple, palaces, ministries and major landmarks.

Grand Palace
Bangkok's major landmark, the Grand Palace is a walled city founded in 1782 by King Rama I and gradually enlarged by subsequent Chakri monarchs. The complex contains royal household offices, the Chakri Hall, a striking example of Italian architecture surmounted by a Thai roof, lesser buildings, and the dazzling Wat Phra Kaeo (Emerald Buddha Chapel) which houses Thailand's most revered image.

The Palace complex is open daily 8.30am–11.30am and 1–4pm, excluding holidays, and there is no entrance fee on Sat or Sun.

Visitors are requested to wear suitable clothing for visiting a king, although he no longer lives there, so no shorts or bare shoulders will be admitted.

On the left-hand side, after entering the palace, there is a gate leading to Wat Phra Keo, which was the private temple of the king.

Chakri Maha Prasad is the main building, and is a mixture of Thai and Victorian architecture. In this is the throne room, which is not open to the public. Then there are the reception rooms furnished with memoriabilia of various state visits, which the public are welcome to visit.

On the right-hand side of Chakri Maha Prasad is Dusit Maha Prasad, which was built during the reign of Rama I in the 18th century. This is where the investiture of Rama VI took place.

Amarin Vinachai Hall, the old High Court of Justice, is to the left, and was also built in the 18th century. Coronation ceremonies are traditionally held here. The two red posts at the front were for tethering the royal elephant so the king could climb aboard.

Also in the complex are the old Royal Harem and Borompiman Hall, neither of which are open to the public.

Most westerners will relate to the palace as the setting for the book "Anna And The King Of Siam", and more recently the movie "The King And I", but apart from showing a blackboard in one of the rooms which may, or may not, have been used by Anna to teach the king's children, the Thai people really do not want to talk about the story. If you persevere, they will tell you that there was a lady called Anna, and some of her descendants still live in Bangkok, but that most of the story was fiction.

While walking through the grounds, take note of the pot plants, some of which are actually bonsai believed to be about 400 hundred years old.

Wat Phra Keo (Temple of the Emerald Buddha)
The most venerated temple in all Thailand, Wat Phra Keo is the home of the Emerald Buddha, which dates back to the 15th century when it was found after a small pagoda at Chiang Rai was struck by lightning. The Buddha was originally covered in stucco, which wore off over a period of time, revealing a deep green statue covered in pure jasper.

Fishing on the Chao Phraya River

Sukhothai

Buddhist Monks

The statue is housed in the royal chapel of the temple, and it really is beautiful, but I must admit that after hearing so much about it, especially in Thailand, I expected something much bigger. To save you that disappointment — the statue is only 65 cm (26 in) tall. It is placed under a huge parasol, and has three different sets of clothes — gold for the hot season, diamonds for the cold season and blue spangles for the rainy season.

Surrounding the royal chapel is the cloister, with galleries adorned with frescoes illustrating the Ramakien and the exploits of Hanuman, the monkey-god. These date from the late 18th century, and have been well looked after, and are regularly restored.

The temple is open daily 8.30am–11.30am and 1pm–3.30pm, and there is no entrance fee on Sun and Buddhist holidays.

The National Museum
The museum is a mixture of old and new buildings, and contains everything there is to know about Thai Art. It is situated in Na Phra That Road, ph 224 1396, and is closed Mon and Fri, open other days from 9am–4pm. Guided tours are conducted Wed and Thurs at 9.30am, lasting about 2 hours.

Wat Po (Temple of the Reclining Buddha)
Close to Wat Phra Keo, this is Bangkok's largest and oldest temple, and was built in the 16th century. The buildings of the complex are situated around two courtyards, and there are 16 entrances, but only 2 are open to the public.

The main building is The Bot, surrounded by two galleries which have 394 seated Buddhas.

The Reclining Buddha is thought to be about 44 m (145 ft) long and 15 m (50 ft) high, though some experts disagree as to its size. The disappointing part of viewing it is that it is in a room that is not much bigger than the statue, so it is impossible to step back and place it in perspective. Essentially, all that can be seen are the soles of the feet, which are covered with mother-of-pearl, illustrating the marks and qualities of Buddha.

The southern part of the temple is a monastic township, with about 300 monks in residence in Thai houses. It is easy to talk a monk into giving you a guided tour.

Other outstanding temples include Wat Saket (with the Golden

Mount), Wat Suthat (with the Giant Swing), Wat Traimit (with a solid gold Buddha weighing five and a half tons), Wat Arun (Temple of Dawn) whose central tower, encrusted with statuary of mythological beings, soars some 75 m above the river, and Wat Benchamabophit (Marble Temple).

Wiman Mek Palace
This was the favourite residence of King Chulalongkorn (1868–1910), and is the world's largest golden teak building.

✗ Pasteur Institute's Snake Farm
Here cobras and kraits are fed daily and 'milked' for venom to make invaluable serum.

Jim Thompson's Thai House
An architect from New York, Jim Thompson came to Thailand at the end of the Second World War, and became interested in the silk industry, making Thai silk a household word. The house, situated at Soi Kasemsan 2, in front of the National Stadium, is open Mon–Fri, 9.30am–4pm. There is an entry fee, all proceeds go to charity.

There are actually six houses, which are all authentic, as they have been brought, dismantled, from different parts of Thailand, and rebuilt here.

Suan Pakkad Palace
This palace, at 352 Si Ayutthaya Road, is the home of Princess Chumbot, and is open to the public Mon–Sat, 9am–4pm. There is an entry fee. The palace is well worth a visit to see the collections of her late husband, Prince Chumbot. The 'piece de resistance' is a lacquerwork pavilion, decorated with 17th century gold leaf murals, which was originally from a temple near Ayutthaya, and restored by the Prince.

✗ The Floating Market
The well-known Wat Sai Talat can hardly be classed as a market anymore, more like a series of boutiques and specialty shops. Still it is worth a visit because of the insight into the life of the people who live on the canals (klongs). It is not your normal suburban

scene, and can be a bit of a culture shock. Tours can be arranged by local travel agencies, or catch a boat from the pier near the Oriental Hotel.

OUTLYING ATTRACTIONS

Crocodile Farm
Near the Chao Phraya's estuary at Samut Prakan, 30 km (18 miles) south-east of Bangkok, is the world's largest crocodile farm. Of course, it is best to visit at feeding time, but if that is not possible still go because there is always some action as these creatures don't always get on together very well, and fights break out all the time. Ph 395 1477 for organised tours.

If you are the type who has to experience everything, here is a chance to sample crocodile meat at the restaurants in Samut Prakan — not everybody's cup of tea.

The Ancient City
This 80 ha (200 acres) open-air museum has authentic reproductions of architectural forms — temples, palaces, shrines, rural dwellings — from each of Thailand's 73 provinces. It is situated 33 km (20 miles) south-west of Bangkok, a short distance from the Crocodile Farm. Ph 221 4495 for information.

Rose Garden
A riverside tropical park-cum-country club, the Rose Garden is 32 km (20 miles) west of Bangkok on the Nakhon Pathom Road. It features a Thai Village with a cultural performance every afternoon at 2.15pm and 3.15pm. OK it's very commercial, but it is a really entertaining show, with exhibitions of traditional dancing, kick fighting, sabre fencing and cock fighting. The 'natives' who take part in the show are obviously not just dragged in off the street, they are professionals, but you get an idea of how it was in days gone by, so does it really matter?

Of course there are rose bushes, about 20,000 of them, as well as an 18-hole championship golf course and all types of recreational activities and water sports. There is also bungalow accommodation available. And like every other tourist spot in the world, there are shops selling souvenirs and artifacts.

If you arrive at the Rose Garden by bus, unknown to you

someone will take your photo as you get out of the bus, then when you return you will have the chance to buy it — on a china plate.

For information ph 251 1935–6.

Nakhom Pathom

This little town, 56 km (35 miles) south-west of Bangkok, hosts the world's tallest Buddhist monument, the orange-tiled Phra Pathom Chedi. The monument marks the spot where Buddhism was introduced some 2,300 years ago to the Thailand-to-be.

Damnoen Saduak

Thailand's most vibrant floating market, Damnoen Saduak is 80 km (50 miles) south-west of Bangkok in the province of Ratchabur. The market is open every day until noon, and farmers congregate to sell fresh produce. A visit to this market is like a step back in time and should not be missed.

Wat Phailom

This temple is on the east bank of the Chao Phraya in Pathum Thani province, some 20 km (12 miles) north of Bangkok, and is a sanctuary for open-bill storks. Between December and June, thousands of storks nest in the temple area.

Bang Sai Folk Arts & Crafts Centre

The riverside Bang Sai Folk Arts & Crafts Centre is some 30 km (19 miles) upstream from Bangkok, and enjoys royal patronage. It offers immaculately handcrafted products.

Bang Pa-In

About 50 km (31 miles) north of Bangkok, Bang Pa In is the site of the summer residence of the kings of Ayutthaya. It was destroyed by the Burmese, and the present buildings date from the late 19th century.

The Park is open Mon–Sat, 8.30am–3.30pm, and there is an entrance fee.

There is a lake with an island, on which stands the Aisawan Thi Paya, the best pavilion in this complex, and a fine example of Thai architecture. It contains a statue of King Chulalongkorn, who was a regular visitor. Incidentally, there is a sad story concerning his wife — she drowned here in full view of a retinue of servants, who could not save her because of an old rule forbidding them to touch a royal person.

The royal palace consists of five buildings, built in Thai, Chinese, Italian and Victorian styles.

In the centre of the grounds is the Wehat Chamrun (Chinese Pavilion) which was presented to the king by the Chinese community of·Thailand in gratitude for their welcome into the country.

Ayutthaya
This sleepy riverine island town, 86 km (53 miles) north of Bangkok, was the Siamese capital from 1350 to 1767 when it was sacked by invading Burmese. Magnificent ruins of palaces, temples and crumbling fortresses provide eloquent testimony of the former capital's splendour.

TOURS
Many economical tours are offered by large travel agencies, several of which operate desks in leading hotels. Smaller agencies customarily operate from economy-class hotels or neighbouring streets. Visitors seeking detailed information on such tours are advised to contact the Association of Thai Travel Agents, 94 Soi Langsuan, Ploenchit Road, Bangkok, ph 252 0069.

Here are a few examples.

Half Day Tours around Bangkok

Grand Palace
Visit the Grand Palace, Coronation Hall, Throne Hall, Reception Hall and the compound of Wat Phra Kaeo (Emerald Buddha Temple) — US$10–20.

Temples and City
Visit three most interesting temples; Golden Buddha, Reclining Buddha; Marble Temple, and short city tour — US$9–19.

Ancient City
Visit many authentically reconstructed and historically significant monuments and temples of Thailand. Large outdoor museum portrays the evolution and the survival of the Thai culture and art — US$12–27.

Crocodile Farm
One of the world's largest crocodile farms, with a small zoo — US$11–25.

Rose Garden/Thai Village Show
Beautiful surroundings, lively folk show, and elephants at work — US$14–29.

National Museum
The largest museum in South-east Asia, housing objects of great significance — US$11–19.

Floating Market at Bangkok
Boat trip along the Chao Phraya River and canals passing scenes of typical Thai life before visiting the Floating Market and Wat Arun, the Temple of Dawn — US$10–25.

Damnoen Saduak Floating Market
Visit the most colourful and largest floating market in Thailand at Damnoen Saduak. On the return trip visit the largest pagoda at Nakhon Pathom — US$21–38.

Rice Barge Cruise (incl. snacks and beverages)
By long-tailed boats and rice barge through rural canals to an ancient and simple way of life of the real Thailand — US$13–29.

Floating Market combined with either Grand Palace or Temple and City Tour
Boat ride passing Floating Market and Wat Arun. Continue by car/coach to visit either the Grand Palace or two other famous temples — rates on application.

Thai Mon Twilight
Drive to the Oriental Pier, continue by motorboat two hours up the Chao Phraya River to Nonthaburi Province. Enroute visit Wat Chaloemprakiat, Wat Porramai and pottery factory on Ko (island) Kret. Dinner at the Riverside Restaurant while watching the traditional dancing of the Mons. Return by boat to the Oriental Pier — rates on application.

Bangkok City Tour
By air-conditioned bus, visiting Pasteur Institute's snake farm, Wat Benchamabophit (the marble temple). Driving around the

city to see Lumphini Park, Chulalongkorn Hospital and University, the former Parliament Building (stopping to see the Marble Throne Hall), the Golden Mount temple and ancient walled city area — rates on application.

Jim Thompson's House and Suan Pakkard Palace
Visit the famous house of Thailand's late Thai silk king, Jim Thompson and unique Lacquer Pavilion at Suan Pakkard Palace — US$13–28.

Full Day Tours from Bangkok

River Cruise to Ayutthaya
By Oriental Queen cruise along the Chao Phraya Rver, visit Bang Pa-In Summer Palace and the ancient city of Ayutthaya (lunch aboard) — US$25–78.

Ancient Capital of Ayutthaya
A drive through rural areas exploring the old Summer Palace at Bang Pa-In with its old buildings and pavilions and then to Ayutthaya itself. Visit Hualaem Village, famous for its products made from palm leaves. Then to Ban Mai Village for wood-carved products — US$20–46.

Damnoen Saduak and River Kwai
To the floating market at Damnoen Saduak. Visit also the Bridge over the River Kwai and the War Cemetery of Allied Soldiers. On the way back visit Nakhon Pathom to explore the highest pagoda in the world — US$27–55.

Mahachai Fishing Village by Boat and Train
After a 3-hour scenic boat trip on a Klong (canal) you reach the busy fishing village of Mahachai. Visit large markets and enjoy a splendid fish lunch. Exciting train trip back to Bangkok — rates on application.

RIVER AND KLONG TRIPS

Thai rivers and klongs have always been vital forms of communication and in the 19th century, Bangkok was laced with canals, giving the capital the name, the 'Venice of the East'. The following trips are highly recommended.

Express Boat Trip from Bangkok to Nonthaburi
An express boat service on the Chao Phraya river connects Bangkok with the northern neighbouring province of Nonthaburi, beginning from the Wat Rajsingkon Pier near the Krung Thep Bridge. The fare is 7 baht. Major sights along the route are the Memorial Bridge, Wat Arun (Temple of Dawn), the riverine walled city, the Grand Palace and Thammasat University. The most convenient places to board the boat are at the Tha Chang Pier near the Grand Palace, or Tha Phra Chan Pier near Thammasat University. The service operates daily, 6am–6pm.

Trip to Klong Bang Waek
Boats leave Bangkok's Memorial Bridge Pier every 15 minutes, 6am–5pm. The single fare is 4 baht. Scenic attractions include canalside temples and orchid farms.

Trip to Klong Mon
Boats leave every 30 minutes, 6.30am–6pm, from Bangkok's Tha Tien Pier behind Wat Pho (Temple of the Reclining Buddha). The single fare is 4 baht. The picturesque trip features canalside temples, orchards, orchid farms and fascinating vignettes of waterborne life.

Trip to Klong Bang Khoo Wiang and Klong Bang Yai
Leaving from the Tha Chang Pier near the Grand Palace, every 20 minutes, 6.15am–8pm, this trip costs 10 baht per person. Attractions include waterside temples, Thai-style houses, the Royal Barge Museum and Khoo Wiang Floating Market, which is open between 4 and 7am.

Trip to Klong Om
Boats leave every 15 minutes from Nonthaburi's Phibul Songkram Pier, 4am–9pm. Scenic attractions include temples, Thai-style houses and durian plantations.

Klong Pravate Tour
A daily 3–7pm boat trip on Klong Pravate is organised by East-West Tours Co., Ltd., for 270 baht per person. The price includes

drinks, snacks, and stopover at a Thai house to watch a demonstration of rural Thai activities. For information and reservations, ph 253 0681–6.

Chao Phraya River Dinner Cruise

The Oriental Hotel organises a dinner aboard a luxury river cruiser travelling between the hotel and the Rama VI Bridge every Wednesday, 8–10pm. The cost of 480 baht per person includes dinner. For information and reservations, ph 236 0400–9.

The Loy Nava Co., Ltd., also provides a dinner cruise, twice daily between 6–8pm and 8–10pm between the River City Pier and Wasukri Pier. The 400 baht per person cost includes dinner. For information and reservations, ph 437 4932, 437 7329.

Cruise to Ayutthaya

The Oriental Queen river cruiser leaves the Oriental Hotel at 8am every day, arriving in the former Siamese capital at 12.30pm. Visitors are taken by air-conditioned bus to see the former capital's ruins and Bang Pa-In Summer Palace. The same coach returns to Bangkok at 5pm. The cost of 740 baht per person includes lunch. For information and reservations, ph 236 0400–9.

Budget Package Boat Trips

The Chao Phraya Express Boat Co., Ltd., provides tour programmes along the Chao Phraya River to Bang Pa-In; Nonthaburi's Tan Noi Garden; the Thai Folk Arts and Handicrafts Centre in Bang Si; Wat Phai Lom, with its sanctuary for open-billed storks; and Wat Phai Rong Woa with its large Buddha image. The tour is operated every Saturday, Sunday and official holidays. For information and reservations, ph 222 5330, 410 1305. The price is 140 baht per person.

Suggested 7-Day Itinerary

Day One

Morning visit to Grand Palace, Wat Phra Kaeo, Wat Pho and Lak Muang shrine. Afternoon boat trip exploring Bangkok's west-bank canals and orchards.

Evening — Thai dinner and classical dance performance.

Day Two
Morning visit to Jim Thompson's Thai House. Afternoon visit to
Wiman Mek Palace, the world's largest golden teak building.
  Evening — Dinner cruise along the Chao Phraya river.

Day Three
Full-day trip to visit The Ancient City (morning) and the Croco-
dile Farm (afternoon).
  Evening — Leisure/nightlife in the Phatphong area.

Day Four
Morning visit to Pasteur Institute Snake Farm to watch snakes
being fed and venom extracted, and Suan Pakkad Palace. Afternoon of leisure, or shopping.
  Evening — Thai boxing at one of Bangkok's three stadiums.

Day Five
Full-day trip to Damnoen Saduak Floating Market, Nakhon
Pathom and the Rose Garden to enjoy cultural show at the Thai
Village.
  Evening — Leisure.

Day Six
Morning departure by coach to Bang Pa-In Summer Palace,
ancient capital of Ayutthaya, afternoon return to Bangkok by river
cruiser along 'The River of Kings'.
  Evening — Leisure.

Day Seven
Morning visit to Wat Benchamabophit, Golden Mount and Wat
Traimit. Afternoon relaxation at Siam Water Park's artificial sea
and water gardens.
  Evening — Leisure.

SPORT AND RECREATION

Golf
Army Golf Course, 25 minutes from the city centre, off the main
highway to the international airport. Contact address: 459 Ram
Inthra Road, Bang Khen, Bangkok, ph 521 1530. 6,650 yards,
par 72. Open daily 6am–6pm.

Green fees — weekdays 120 baht; weekends 250 baht.
Caddy fee — 90 baht.
Clubs for hire — 250 baht.

Krungthep Sports Golf Club, 30 minutes from Bangkok, next to the Unico Golf Course. Contact address: 516 Krungthem Kritha Road, Hua Mark, Bang Kabi, Bangkok, ph 374 0491. 6,712 yards, par 72. Open daily 6am–6pm.

Green fees — weekdays 250 baht; weekends 500 baht.
Caddy fee — 100 baht.

Railway Training Centre Golf Course, 15 minutes from the city centre. Contact address: Vibhavadi Rangsit Road, Bang Khen, Bangkok, ph 271 0130. 6,775 yards, par 72. Open daily 6am–6pm.

Green fees — weekdays 140 baht (special fee after 3pm); weekends 260 baht.
Caddy fee — 150 baht.
Clubs for hire — 200 baht.

Royal Thai Air Force Golf Course, Don Muang, Bangkok. Contact address: Royal Thai Air Force, Vibhavadi Rangsit Road, Bang Khen, Bangkok, ph 523 6103. 4,300 yards, par 68. Open daily 7am–6pm.

Green fees — weekdays 100 baht; weekends 150 baht (special fee after 3pm all days).
Caddy fee — 50 baht.
Clubs for hire — 200 baht.

Unico Golf Course, 520 Hua Mak, Bangkok. Contact address: 47 Mu 7, Krungthep Kritha Road, Prawet, Phra Khanong, Bangkok, ph 377 9038. 6,527 yards, par 72. Open daily 6am–6pm.

Green fees — weekdays 160 baht (special fee after 3pm); weekends 320 baht.
Caddy fee — 100 baht.
Clubs for hire — 200 baht.

Rose Garden Golf Course, Nakhon Pathom, ph 253 0295. Contact address: 459 Ram Inthra Road, Bang Khen, Bangkok, ph 521 1530. 6,435 yards, par 72. Open Tues–Sun 6am–6pm.

Green fees — weekdays 180 baht (special fee after 3pm); weekends 380 baht.
Caddy fee — 100 baht.
Clubs for hire — 200 baht.

Navatanee Golf Course, 30 minutes from centre of Bangkok. Contact address: 22 Mu 1, Sukhaphiban 2 Road, Bang Kapi, Bangkok, ph 372 6127, 374 7077. 6,241 yards, par 72. Open 6am–6pm.

> Green fees — weekdays 300 baht (ladies 200 baht); weekends 750 baht.
> Caddy fee — 120 baht (girl caddies).
> Clubs for hire — 300 baht.

Ekachai Golf Course, Samut Sakhon, 40 minutes' drive west of Bangkok. Contact address: 2013 Italthai House, New Phetburi Road, Bangkok, ph 314 0392. 6,131 yards, par 72. Open 6am–6pm.

> Green fees — weekdays 150 baht; weekends 300 baht.
> Caddy fee — 100 baht.
> Clubs for hire — 250 baht.

Muang-Ake Golf Course, 40 minutes from city centre, 5 minutes from international airport. Contact address: 34 Mu 7, Phahon-yothin Road, Amphoe Muang, Pathum Thani, ph 533 9336–7–8. 6,211 yards, par 72. Open 6am–6pm.

> Green fees — weekdays 150 baht (after 3.30pm 100 baht); weekends 300 baht (after 3.30pm 150 baht).
> Caddy fee — 100 baht.
> Clubs for hire — 200 baht.

Royal Dusit Golf Course, at the Royal Turf Club — closed on race days. Contact address: Phitsanulok Road, Dusit, Bangkok, ph 281 4320. 4,919 yards, par 66. Open 6am–6pm.

> Green fees — weekdays 120 baht; weekends 200 baht.
> Caddy fee — 50 baht.
> Clubs for hire — 200 baht.

Panya Resort Golf Course 82.5 km (51 miles) from Bangkok on the Bang Na-Trat Highway. Contact address: Panya Resort Co., Ltd., 204 Panya Village, Phatthanakan Road, Phra Khanong, Bangkok, ph 314 0571–3. 3 courses (A/B/C/), par 72. A/B 7,009 yards, A/C 7,006 yards, B/C 6,963 yards. Open 6am–6pm.

> Green fees — weekdays 300 baht; weekends and holidays 500 baht.
> Caddy fees — 9 holes 100 baht; 18 holes 150 baht.
> Clubs for hire — 150 baht.

Horse Racing
Weekend races, each card averaging 10 races, can be seen at Bangkok's Royal Turf Club, Phitsanulok Road, and Royal Bangkok Sports Club, Henri Dunant Road.

Tennis/Badminton/Squash
Numerous opportunities are found in leading Bangkok hotels.

Thai Boxing
Ratchadamnoen Stadium — Mon, Wed, Thurs, Sat.
Lumphini Stadium — Tues, Fri, Sat.

Thai currency

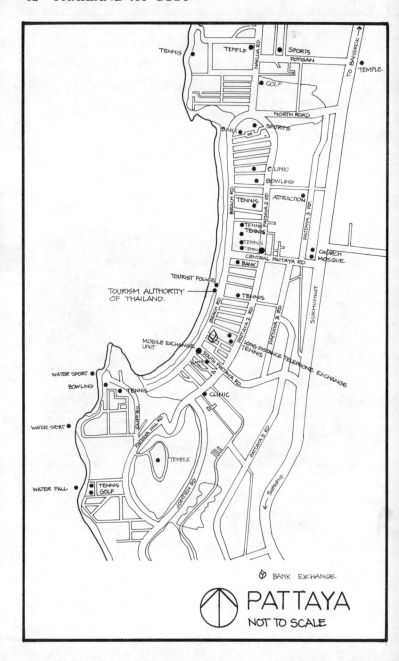

BANK EXCHANGE

PATTAYA
NOT TO SCALE

PATTAYA

Pattaya is Asia's premier beach resort and annually attracts millions of pleasure-seekers from all over the world.

Its sunny world is synonymous with pleasant beaches, every conceivable water sport from windsurfing to scuba diving, alluring off-shore coral islands, excellent accommodation lining the resort's palm-fringed crescent bay, superb seafood, a colourful, relaxing tropical ambience and, after sunset, a seedy nightlife.

HOW TO GET THERE
Pattaya is 147 km (91 miles) south-east of Bangkok, a 2 hour drive along Highway No. 3 via Bang Na, Bang Pakong, Chon Buri and Siracha.

Air-conditioned and non-air-conditioned coaches regularly leave Bangkok's Eastern Bus Terminal, at the mouth of Soi Ekamai (Soi 63) on Sukhumwit Road, throughout the day.

There are no rail or air services linking Bangkok and Pattaya.

TOURIST INFORMATION
The Tourism Authority of Thailand has an office at 382/1 Chaihat Road, South Pattaya, ph (038) 428 750, 429 113. Next door is the Tourist Police Centre.

ACCOMMODATION
As expected at such a tourist resort, there is a wide choice in the way of accommodation. Here we have listed a selection, with prices for a double room per night in bahts. Again we stress, these prices should be used as a guide only. The Telephone Area Code is 038.

Deluxe Hotels
Royal Cliff Beach Resort, 378 Pratamnak Road, Pattaya City, ph 421 421. The ultimate in resort hotels, the Royal Cliff has over 700

guest rooms, many with ocean views. Apart from the elevator down to its private beach, the hotel has 2 swimming pools, 24-hour coffee shop, grill room, supper club, 3 bars, shopping arcade, health club, 6 tennis courts and equipment for all forms of water sports — 2,662 baht.

Royal Garden Resort, 218 Beach Road, Pattaya City, ph 428 126. Situated at the southern end of Pattaya Beach, close to the shopping and entertainment centre, the hotel has 164 guest rooms, most with balconies and water views. Facilities include a swimming pool with adjoining kiddies' pool, 2 tennis courts, the Hideaway Seafood restaurant, coffee shop, the Garden Sidewalk Cafe, disco and shopping arcade — 1,815 baht.

Siam Bayshore, 559 Mu 10, South Pattaya, ph 428 678. The resort is set in over 8ha (20 acres) of tropical parkland, and has 274 guest rooms. There are 3 restaurants, a nightclub, 2 swimming pools, 4 tennis courts, bars, and equipment for all water sports — 1,547 baht.

Siam Bayview, Pattaya Beach, ph 428 678. One of the newest hotels in Pattaya, it has 260 guest rooms, and is within walking distance of the shopping and entertainment centre of Pattaya. There are three restaurants, 24-hour coffee shop, 2 swimming pools with snack bars and bars — 2,057–2,420 baht.

First Class Hotels

Asia Pattaya, 253 Cliff Road, Pattaya City, ph 428 602. Built on a cliff overlooking a private beach, the hotel is about 8 minutes from the centre of town and has 314 guest rooms. Facilities include 5 restaurants, 3 bars and supper club, swimming pool, games room, tennis court, 9-hole golf course, water sports equipment and shopping arcade — 1,694 baht.

Dusit Resort, 240 Pattaya Beach Road, ph 429 901. The resort, situated at the northern end of Pattaya Beach, opened in December 1988, and has 500 guest rooms. There are 2 restaurants, coffee shop, cocktail lounge, 2 swimming pools, fitness centre, 3 tennis courts, and equipment for all water sports — 1,600–2,000 baht.

Merlin Pattaya, Pattaya Beach Road, ph 428 755. The hotel has 360 guest rooms, a restaurant, bar, coffee shop, snooker club, tennis

Koh Rang Nok, Tarutao

Sofitel Central, Hua Hin

Phimai Temple, Nakhon Ratchasima

court, 9-hole golf course, videotheque and shopping arcade — 1,400 baht.

Montein Pattaya, 369 Mu 9, Pattaya Klang Road, ph 428 155. The sister hotel of the Montien in Bangkok, this hotel has 300 guest rooms, all with private balconies and water views. Facilities include a swimming pool, 2 tennis courts, games room, 24-hour coffee shop, 3 restaurants, cocktail lounge, nightclub and shopping arcade — 1,750–2,800 baht.

Nipa Lodge, Pattaya Beach, ph 428 195. Situated about 5 minutes' walk from the beach, this friendly hotel has 147 guest rooms, a restaurant, bar, coffee shop, tennis court, swimming pool, night club and shopping arcade — 1,452 baht.

Orchid Lodge, 240 Mu 5, Pattaya-Naklua Road, ph 428 161. Set in 4ha (10 acres) of landscaped gardens leading down to the beach frontage, the hotel has 236 guest rooms and 2 swimming pools, 2 tennis courts, mini-golf course, 3 restaurants, coffee shop, disco, and scuba diving gear — 1,400 baht.

Royal Cruise Hotel, 499 North Pattaya Beach Road, ph 424 242. A new hotel with a difference! It's built in the shape of a luxury cruise liner, and its 200 guest rooms are called cabins. Facilities are what you would expect — swimming pool, health club, restaurant, coffee shop and a pub/bar — 2,200 baht.

Standard Hotels

Diamond Beach, 373/8 South Pattaya Beach Road, ph 429 885 — 138 guest rooms — restaurant, bar, coffee shop, health club, snooker club, swimming pool, videotheque and shopping arcade — 800 baht.

Ocean View, 283 Mu 10, Beach Road, South Pattaya, ph 428 084 — 112 guest rooms — restaurant, bar, coffee shop, swimming pool and shopping arcade — 1,261 baht.

Prima Villa, 157/22-23 Pattaya-Naklua Road, ph 425 706 — bar, coffee shop, snookerclub, swimming pool, videotheque and shopping arcade — 726 baht.

Seaview Resort, 500 soi 18, Pattaya-Naklua Road, ph 429 317 — 242 guest rooms — restaurant, bar, coffee shop, snooker club, swimming pool, nightclub and shopping arcade — 968 baht.

LOCAL TRANSPORT

Mini-buses perpetually complete counter-clockwise circuits around the Beach Road and Pattaya 2 Road. Fares are 5 baht. Fares beyond the main bay area are negotiable.

Cars, jeeps and motorcycles are widely available on a daily self-drive basis.

EATING OUT

Seafood is the main item on every restaurant menu. One place, Nang Nual in south Pattaya has about 200 different seafood dishes.

The cuisine in the hotels is more varied, with Polynesian, French and Italian dishes on offer. The food in the hotels is excellent, if a little pricy.

There are many restaurants, and it is best to check them out during the day to make sure you'll get what you want for the price you are willing to pay.

ENTERTAINMENT

Major hotels have gourmet restaurants, cocktail lounges, discotheques, nightclubs and supper clubs which offer excellent food, drinks, music and entertainment. Such establishments are usually suitable for family entertainment.

Beyond the hotels, discotheques, cabarets, nightclubs, coffee shops, open-air bars, massage parlours and restaurants with live music and entertainment compete for attention.

Such establishments are located mostly along the beach and in South Pattaya.

Don't wander around Pattaya at night with your pockets over-flowing, as someone will probably lighten your load. Best to leave your valuables in the hotel safe deposit box.

SHOPPING

Along the beach and in South Pattaya, there are literally hundreds of little shops selling gems, jewellery, silk and cotton handicrafts, souvenirs, films, tapes, pharmaceuticals and liquor. There are quite a few tailors ready to make your outfit in a day or so.

There are also several shops where you can wait and watch a Rembrandt, or a Gauguin being copied with a great deal of skill by local artists. The prices are quite reasonable, and the finished product would be a great talking point back home.

I found Pattaya the best place in Thailand to buy precious stones, and the variety of settings in rings, ear-rings and necklaces is staggering. Of course, make sure that the store where you find that 'special something' has the blue Tourism Authority of Thailand emblem in its window.

If you are interested in dress lengths, there are many places offering hand-painted fabrics, which are inexpensive and really exquisite.

The shops are open till quite late at night.

SIGHTSEEING

Pattaya is predominately a beach resort, and there are unlimited opportunities to windsurf, waterski, parasail, swim, fish, sunbathe, sail and snorkel. There are also trips on offer to off-shore islands, all year round, to explore some of Asia's finest scuba-diving waters.

Visitors can rent water scooters to explore Pattaya bay, and motorcycles and jeeps to explore neighbouring beaches, particularly those south of Pattaya — Chomthian Beach, Golden Beach, Sunset Beach where accommodation is also available — to Bang Sare fishing village.

Inland, they can visit orchid farms, botanical gardens and parks, or drive through orchards, plantations and undulating countryside surrounding Pattaya.

There are also several Buddhist temples to visit, including the unusual Wat Yansangworararam.

Pattaya Park

A water amusement park located beside Chomthian Beach features water slides and whirlpools, and has some accommodation.

Pattaya Elephant Kraal

Every afternoon this complex has an entertaining show, featuring exhibitions of obedience, strength and forestry skills of the elephants, and shows them bathing in the creek. Of course, elephants don't have an attractive scent, but don't let that put you off.

There is usually one cheeky baby elephant which will keep everybody amused, and the animals are really quite tame. After the show you can climb on board if you like, but remember you will be a long way off the ground.

Nong Nooch Village
A 243 ha (600 acre) country resort 15 minutes south of Pattaya, this village features orchid nurseries, an arts and crafts centre and a cultural show of folk dances, traditional ceremonies and martial arts displays.

OUTLYING ATTRACTIONS
Pattaya is the ideal base for exploring Thailand's east coast. From Pattaya, heading south-east, the attractions are:

Bang Saen
106 km (65 miles) east of Bangkok, Bang Saen is the closest beach resort to the capital. It has a long beach, several fine restaurants and a magnificent marine aquarium. There are several boat tours available from here, and tours to neighbouring fishing villages.

Khao Khiao Open Zoo
This 486 ha (1,200 acre) park houses Asian, African and European mammals and contains Thailand's most spectacular aviary.

Siracha
A seaside town which is well-known for fine seafood served with a delicious local sauce.

Bang Sare
This fishing village is the setting off point for local and international game fisherman to fish the waters of the Gulf.

Samet Island
Rayong's beautiful island is blessed with some of the eastern Gulf's loveliest beaches and snorkelling waters. Rayong is 179 km (111 miles) from Bangkok.

Chanthaburi
This area, 245 km (152 miles) from Bangkok, is well-known for gemstones, particularly sapphires, tropical fruits, waterfalls, historic sites and Thailand's largest Christian church.

Trat
Thailand's eastern most coastal province, Trat borders Kampuchea

and contains a 51-island Marine National Park dominated by the mountainous Ko Chang, Thailand's third largest island. Trat is 315 km (195 miles) from Bangkok.

TOURS
There are several local tours available, and for information and bookings enquire at your hotel information desk, or at the local office of the Tourism Authority of Thailand, ph 428 750, 429 113.

Coral Islands
A boat cruise of Pattaya Bay to the offshore islands, noted for their vivid coral formations and colourful tropical fish. Lunch inclusive — US$17–27.

Sapphire Mine Tour
Visit to mining fields near Chanthaburi, where sapphires, topazes and spinel rubies are found, and the Phriu Waterfalls and Khai Noen Wong fortification. Visit Ban-Phe fishing village, rubber, plantation, King Taksin Fort. Lunch inclusive — US$35–40.

Paradis Island Tour
Depart from Pattaya for one hour drive south to Rayong, visit typical Thai fishing village and community followed by half hour trip on Thai sailing junk to an unspoilt mystery island — rates on application.

Pattaya Countryside
Depart for Chachoengsao. En route visit the Nong Mon fruit and seafood markets, then on to Thammanimit Temple to see huge Buddha image. Continue drive, with visits to duck farm, pottery factory and Wat Luang, the temple with thousands of bats. Continue trip on a long-tailed speedboat along the Bang Pa Kong River. Visit Wat Sothon Warawihan. On the return route to Pattaya, a brief visit is made to orchid farm in Chon Buri and oyster farm in Sam Muk Hill. Lunch inclusive — rates on application.

Elephant Kraal
See how wild elephants are rounded up, tamed and trained. Also see how the huge elephants are used to pull, carry or push big logs in lumber work — US$14–21.

Pattaya Discovery Tour
To Chittaphawan Buddhist College, orchid farm, stonecutter

village, monkey cliff, marine aquarium and fishing village —
US$13–20.

Nong Nooch Village
A sightseeing tour to Nong Nooch Village, 18 km from Pattaya
Beach Resort, featuring village folk work, orchid nurseries, and
Thai dance presentation — US$12–20.

Suggested 7-Day Itinerary

Day One
Morning departure from Bangkok. Seafood lunch at Bang Saen.
Visit Bang Saen's Marine Science Centre, proceed to Pattaya.
Check-into hotel.
   Evening — orientation/nightlife.

Day Two
Full day of relaxation/exploration/water sports in Pattaya/
Chomthian Beach/Golden Beach/Sunset Beach.
   Evening — leisure/shopping/moonlight trail ride at Reo Park
Ranch.

Day Three
Morning — watersports/golf at Bangphra or Siam Country Club/
relaxation.
   Afternoon visit to Nong Nooch Village for cultural show.
   Evening — leisure.

Day Four
Full-day trip to offshore islands for sightseeing/snorkelling or
scuba-diving or full day fishing expedition from Pattaya or Bang
Sare.
   Evening — leisure.

Day Five
Morning — relaxation/Pattaya Park water garden. Afternoon show
at Pattaya Elephant Kraal.
   Evening — leisure.

Day Six
Full-day return trip to Rayong's Samet Island, picnic lunch,
snorkelling, island walks, swimming, etc.
   Evening — leisure.

Day Seven

Option of a full-day trip to Chanthaburi, or full day of relaxation/ sporting activity at Pattaya beach of preference.

Evening — leisure.

SPORT AND RECREATION

Pattaya's major water sports (entailing rented equipment), and venues, are listed below. For more information enquire at your hotel information desk.

Diving

Dive centres organise daily trips to the off-shore islands of Ko Lan, Ko Sak and Ko Krok, some 45 minutes by boat from the mainland. Here divers can discover interesting coral formations and many special of colourful tropical fish in warm waters ranging in depth from 3 to 25 metres.

There are also trips to wrecks in deeper water at least once a week, or arranged on request. Night dives and extended dive trips are also organised.

A selection of dive centres/schools follows:

Dave's Divers Den, Beach Road, Soi 6, ph 429 382. Contact David Doll or Andy Bennerscheildet. Languages — English and German.

Max's Dive Shop, Nipa Lodge Hotel, ph 428 195. Contact Mrs Max Buchamann. Languages — English, German, French.

Pattaya International Diving Centre, Siam Bayview Hotel, ph 428 728. Contact Tan Day Cheng or Erani Choong.

Reef Dive Shop, Ocean View Hotel, ph 428 084. Contact Sompong Bootsarakamvisithi or James Comes. Languages — English and Thai.

Seafari Sports Center, Royal Garden Resort, ph 428 126–7. Contact Will Burbridge. Languages — English and Thai.

Steve's Dive Shop, Beach Road, Soi 4, ph 428 392. Contact William Steven. Languages — English and Thai.

Trip prices break down into two parts, cost of all day boat trip to different areas, plus cost of any equipment rental. The trip price to the close island group (13 km — 1 hour by boat) is approximately 350 baht. This includes guide, lunch, drink and first aid supplies on board. To this add equipment rental of about 900 baht for 2 dives. The far ring of islands (25–30 km — 2 hours) cost about 550 baht and includes all the same features plus same equipment costs.

Windsurfing

Instruction and rental equipment is available at all major beaches. The best is at Chomthian.

Sailing

Hobie Cats and Prindles are available for rent mainly at Chomthian.

Game Fishing

Fishing expeditions regularly depart from Bang Sare fishing village, some 17 km (11 miles) south of Pattaya, in search of marlin, king mackerel, sharks and barracuda.

Parasailing

Several outfits offering 5–10 minute flights operate on major beaches and Lan Island.

Waterskiing

Speedboats and skis are widely available for rent. Return water-skiing trips to Lan Island are popular.

Pattaya's major land sports, and venues, are as follows:

Golf

Bangphra, a 4 km (2 mile) drive from Km.112 on Highway No. 3. Contact address: 12th floor, Thai Wah Tower, 21 Sathon Tai Road, Yannawa, Bangkok, ph (02) 240 9170–2. Reservations ph (038) 311 149, 311 312. 6,440 yards, par 72. Open 6am–6pm.

   Green fees — weekdays 300 baht; weekends 500 baht.
   Caddy fee — 150 baht.
   Clubs for hire — 250 baht.
   Accommodation — 1,200–1,700 baht.

Siam Country Club, 30 minutes from Pattaya. Contact address: 865 Rama I Road, Pathumwan, Bangkok, ph (02) 215 3124. Reservations ph (038) 418 002. 6,448 yards, par 72. Open 6am–6pm.

Green fees — weekdays 500 baht; weekends 500 baht.
Caddy fee — 100 baht.
Clubs for hire — 150 baht (half set).

Royal Thai Navy Golf Course (Phlu Ta Luang), 30km south of
Pattaya, near the port of Sattahip. Reservations ph (02) 466 1180
ext. Sattahip 2217. 6,800 yards, par 72. Open 6am–6pm.

Green fees — weekdays 120 baht (after 3.30 special fee);
weekends 250 baht.
Clubs for hire — 200 baht.

Horse Riding

The Reo Park Ranch, 5 km (3 miles) from Highway No. 3 along
the Siam Country Club road, offers daytime and enchanting
moonlight trail rides on thoroughbreds imported from Australia.

Car/Motorcycle Racing

The 2.4 km (1.4 miles) Pattaya Circuit, at Km. 14 on Route 36 to
Rayong, regularly features local and international races.

Tennis

Major hotels open their courts to non-guests for a small fee. Some
have resident local professionals who offer hourly instruction.

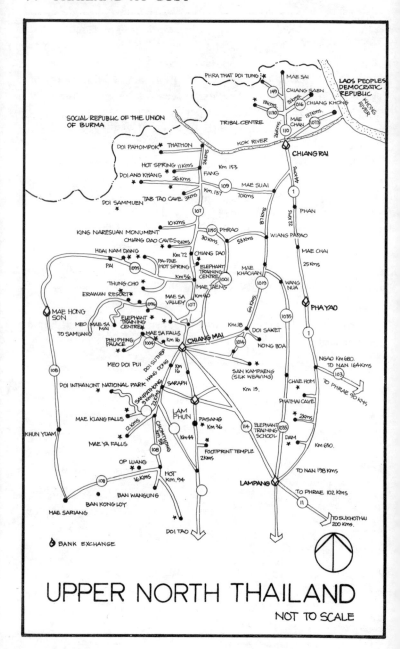

UPPER NORTH THAILAND

NOT TO SCALE

CHIANG MAI

Chiang Mai, Thailands principal northern city, is 696 km (432 miles) north of Bangkok, and is located in a fertile valley 300 m (981 ft) above sea level.

Founded in 1296, it was the capital of Lan Na Thai (Kingdom of One Million Ricefields), the first independent Thai kingdom in the fabled Golden Triangle. Chiang Mai flourished as a major religious, cultural and trading centre until 1556 when a Burmese invasion reduced it to a vassal state. The Burmese were expelled in 1775 and Lan Na Thai once more became part of northern Thailand.

Many lowland Thais regard the city, and province of the same name, as being a national Shangri-la because of the general attractiveness of the women from this area, its distinctive festivals, historic temples dating from the 1300s, arresting scenic beauty, temperate fruits such as apples, peaches and strawberries, and a crisp, invigorating cool season climate.

The mountains surrounding Chiang Mai form the lower extremities of Himalayan foothills and are home to several hill tribes of Tibeto-Burman origin. Forests still worked by elephants, plus an abundance of waterfalls, caves, gorges, cultivated orchards and plantations beckon modern day explorers.

Until the late 1920s, Chiang Mai was isolated from Bangkok and could only be reached by an arduous river trip or by elephant safari through jungled mountains lasting several weeks.

Such isolation accounts for much of Chiang Mai's present charm. The people have their own lilting dialect, customs, handicrafts, architecture, dances and cuisine.

HOW TO GET THERE

By Air
Thai Airways have at least 5 flights a day from Bangkok, with a flying time of one hour.

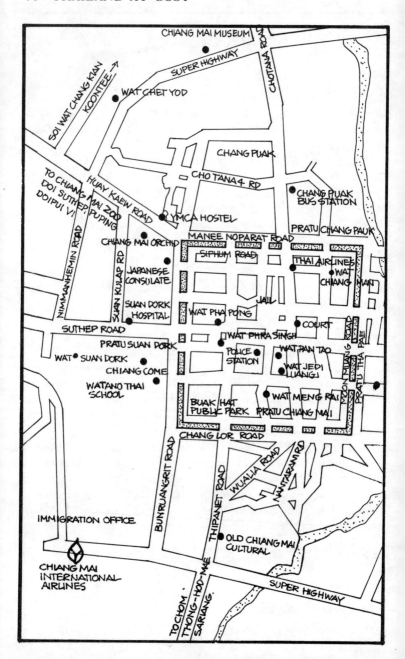

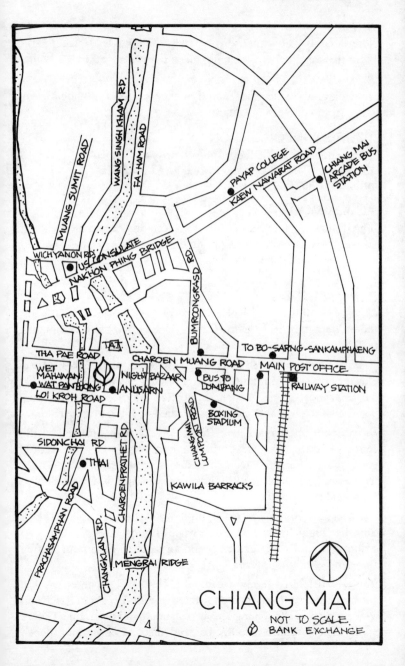

CHIANG MAI

NOT TO SCALE.
BANK EXCHANGE

By Bus
There is a daily bus service from Bangkok's Northern Bus Terminal on Phahonyothin Road, and the trip takes 12 hours.

By Rail
The daily train service from Bangkok's Hualamphong Station takes approximately 14 hours.

TOURIST INFORMATION
The local office of the Tourism Authority of Thailand is situated at 135 Praisani Road, Amphoe Muang, Chiang Mai, ph (053) 235 334.

ACCOMMODATION
The following is a sample of the accommodation available in Chiang Mai. The prices shown are in bahts for a double room per night, and should be used as a guide only. The Telephone Area Code is 053.

First Class Hotels
Chiang Inn, 100 Chang Khlan Road, ph 235 655. With 170 guest rooms, facilities include restaurant, bar, coffee shop, swimming pool, disco and shopping arcade — 1,100 baht.

Chiang Mai Orchid, 100-102 Huay Kaew Road, ph 222 099. A very elegant hotel only 5 minutes' drive from the city centre. The hotel has 265 guest rooms, restaurant, coffee shop, disco, swimming pool, health club and shopping arcade — 1,100–1,600 baht.

Dusit Inn, 112 Chang Khlan Road, ph 251 033. Situated in the centre of Chiang Mai, next to the night markets, the hotel has 200 guest rooms. Facilities include a Chinese restaurant, garden cafe, bar, swimming pool, health club, snooker club and nightclub — 1,815 baht.

Mae Ping, 153 Sridonchai Road, ph 251 060. Located about a block from the night bazaar, the hotel has 374 guest rooms. There is a swimming pool, beer garden, open-air terrace, restaurant, coffee shop and shopping arcade — 1,400 baht.

Rincome, 301 Huay Kaew Road, ph 221 044. The hotel has 158 guest rooms, and has become noted for its excellent food and wine, served in the Thong Kwow restaurant and the Lanna Coffee Shop. There is also a lobby bar and disco, 2 swimming pools, tennis courts and jogging track. Quite close to the hotel is an 18-hole golf course — 1,500 baht.

Superior Hotels

Chiang Mai President, 226 Vichayanon Road, ph 252 050. There are 242 guest rooms and facilities include restaurant, bar, swimming pool and disco — 1,100–1,500 baht.

Chiang Mai Hills, 18 Huay Kaew Road, ph 210 030. Good value hotel with 116 guest rooms, restaurant, bar, coffee shop, health club, swimming pool and shopping arcade — 800 baht.

Diamond, 33/10 Charoenpratet Road, ph 234 155. A small hotel with 145 guest rooms, a restaurant and coffee shop — 800 baht.

Erawan Resort, 30 Mu 2 Tambon Pongyang, ph 251 191. The resort has 59 guest rooms, a restaurant, snooker club and shopping arcade — 800–1,200 baht.

Novotel Suriwongse, 110 Chang Khlan Road, ph 251 051. 168 guest rooms with restaurant, bar, swimming pool and shopping arcade — 1,331 baht.

Standard Hotels

Chiang Come, 7/35 Suthep Road, ph 211 020 — 150 rooms — restaurant and coffee shop — 550–650 baht.

Northern Inn, 234/12 Maneenopparat Road, ph 210 002 — 90 guest rooms — restaurant and coffee shop — 680 baht.

Prince, 3 Taiwang Road, ph 236 744 — 112 guest rooms — restaurant, coffee shop, swimming pool and shopping arcade — 640 baht.

Royal Park, 47 Charoenmuang Road, ph 247 549 — 72 guest rooms — restaurant, bar and swimming pool — 350 baht.

Sri Tokyo, 6 Boonruangrit Road, ph 211 100 — 111 guest rooms — restaurant, bar, coffee shop and swimming pool — 680 baht.

Budget Hotels

Chang Puak, 133 Chotana Road, ph 221 755 — 58 guest rooms — coffee shop — 500 baht.

New Asia, 55 Ratchawong Tadmai Road, ph 235 288 — 204 guest rooms — restaurant — 480 baht.

LOCAL TRANSPORT
Chiang Mai city is compact enough to explore on foot.

Bus
There is an urban bus service, mini-buses which average 5 baht per ride.

Pedicabs (tricycles)
Fares for these must be bargained before setting out.

Car
Cars can be hired on a daily or weekly basis.

EATING OUT
Besides excellent Thai and Chinese food, visitors can enjoy Italian, French, German and Muslim food in specialty restaurants. American-style steakhouses, sandwich bars, fast-food outlets, English-style pubs and vegetarian restaurants offer a broad range of cuisine, and international fare is widely available in teahouses and coffee shops.

Local specialties include highly spiced Naem sausages and mildly curried Khao Soi noodles. Most visitors enjoy a traditional Khantok dinner which is often accompanied by a display of northern dances.

ENTERTAINMENT
Chiang Mai's nightlife is less varied and boisterous than Bangkok's. It revolves mainly around night clubs, discotheques, bars, massage parlours, cocktail lounges, coffee shops, skating rinks and open-air restaurants with singers and live music.

SHOPPING
Chiang Mai is Thailand's major centre for quality handicrafts. There are department stores and night markets with wide ranges of antiques, silver jewellery, hilltribe opium pipes and embroidery, Thai silks and cottons, basketry, celadon, silverware, furniture, lacquerware, wood carvings and parasols.

Central Railway Station, Bangkok

Phuket, one of several First Class Hotels

Tapu Mount, Pang Nga Bay, Southern Thailand

A major advantage of shopping in Chiang Mai is that the visitor can watch artisans working within the city and several outlying villages, particularly along the Bo Sang — San Kamphaeng road.

A soothing bonus, particularly after an extended shopping trip, is to visit San Kamphaeng's Hot Springs (36 km — 22 miles — from town) where water with a high sulphur content is said to possess curative and restorative properties.

SIGHTSEEING

Temples
Northern Thai religious architecture is a flamboyant mixture of Mon, Burmese, Sri Lankan and Lan Na Thai styles. There is a liberal use of accomplished woodcarving, Naga staircases, leonine and angelic guardians, gilded umbrellas and pagodas laced with gold filigree.

Wat Chiang Man
This temple, on Rajpakinai Road, is the oldest in Chiang Mai, and is attributed to Mengrai, the founding king. It is only open on Sundays and Buddhist feast days.

Wat Chedi Luang
Built in 1391, this temple was partially destroyed by earthquake in 1545. It is situated on Pra Pokkiao Road.

Wat Phra Sing
This temple was built in 1345, and its Lai Kham chapel houses the revered Phra Sing Buddha image.

Wat Chet Yot
The Temple of the Seven Spires (Wat Chet Yot) is close to the museum on the Lampang freeway. It was built in the 15th century and modelled on a Burmese pagan temple.

Wat Ku Tao
This temple is worth visiting for its porcelain-studded, exotically bulbous pagoda.

Wat Suan Dok
This temple, on Sutness Road, was built in a 14th century Lan Na Thai king's pleasure gardens. The ashes of the royal family of Chiang Mai are stored here.

Wat Phra That Doi Suthep
Chiang Mai's most important, and visible, temple is 15 km (9 miles) from town, and is a major landmark overlooking the city from its forested mountain backdrop. Thailand's royal family has a winter palace on top of the mountain. The temple's 16th century golden pagoda contains Buddhist relics and attracts pilgrims throughout the year.

12 km (7 miles) along a switchback mountain road, which begins beside the zoo, there is a steep climb up a Naga staircase to the temple's compound from where one has an exhilarating view of Chiang Mai and the surrounding countryside. For the less energetic there are funicular cars.

OUTLYING ATTRACTIONS
Seven major hill tribes, the Meo, Lisu, Lahu, Yao, Akha, Lawa and Karen, live in the mountains of Chiang Mai. The tribes share animist beliefs and honour innumerable forest and guardian spirits. Each has distinctive courtship rituals, games, dances, agricultural customs, puberty rites, languages or dialects, aesthetic values and hygienic habits.

Popular 2 to 7 day 'jungle treks' include visits to remote high-altitude hilltribe settlements and often feature elephant rides. Best guides are hilltribe youths who commonly speak Thai, English and at least three tribal dialects.

You can also visit more accessible hilltribe villages by road, such as during a full-day visit via route 108 to Doi Inthanon National Park (47 km — 29 miles — from town) on Thailand's highest mountain. The Mae Klang, Wachirathan, Siriphum and Mae Pan waterfalls share the mountain with Meo and Karen villages and work elephants, while ferns and lichens decorate the silent forests cloaking the 2,554 m (8,352 ft) summit.

Other hilltribe settlements can be visited along the Mae Sa Valley where major attractions include an Elephant Camp, orchid nurseries, the Mae Sa and Mae Yim waterfalls, and increasingly numerous, landscaped hillside resorts catering to those who want to stay in the hills.

More hilltribe villages can be seen on the highway linking Chiang Dao and Fang. The road passes the Chiang Dao Elephant Camp, the Buddha-image filled caves of Wat Tham Chiang Dao (72 km — 45 miles — from town) and spectacular mountain scenery before entering Fang, known for hot springs and Yao settlements in surrounding mountains.

Neighbouring Provinces

Chiang Mai's central location allows for convenient exploration, either by road or air, of other northern provinces.

These include *Mae Hong Son* 362 km (224 miles) to the west, nestling against the Burmese border with rugged mountain scenery, innumerable hilltribe settlements and Burmese-style temples; *Chiang Rai* 268 km (166 miles) to the north-east, the very heart of the fabled Golden Triangle with majestic mountains and many high-altitude hill tribe villages; *Lampang* 96 km (60 miles) to the south-east, home of many Burmese-style temples and sole remaining provincial capital in Thailand where horse-drawn carriages are used for daily urban transport; and *Lamphun* 26 km (16 miles) to the south, seat of the ancient Hariphunchai kingdom, famous for woven cloth, bountiful lamyai orchards and stunning temples such as Wat Phra That Hariphunchai, a supreme example of classical northern Thai religious architecture.

The Golden Triangle derives its name from two sources: firstly, the shape of the area, with its base as the Burmese-Laotian border and its point at Chiang Rai; and secondly, the massive income from the international sale of opium which is produced in the area.

Chiang Rai is becoming an alternate starting point for hilltribe treks as it is closer to a greater variety of tribes than is Chiang Mai. It also now boasts a new tourist attraction, the Hilltribe Culture and Product Display Centre, which provides a good insight into the tribes. The centre is found at 620/25 Rhanalai Road, and has a hilltribe arts and crafts exhibit and shop on the 2nd floor, and a slide show on the 3rd floor. The slide show is worth a visit, and has narration in English, French, German, Japanese and Thai. The craft exhibit has no admission fee, but the show has a sliding scale of charges from 50 baht for 1 person up to 10 baht each for

10 persons. The centre is run by the Population and Community Development Association (PDA), which is involved in developing hilltribe villages and bringing them into the 20th century. For further information contact the manager of the centre at the above address, or ph 053 713 410.

About 350km (217 miles) south of Chiang Mai is *Sukhothai*, the first capital of Thailand founded in the early 13th century. In Sukhothai Historical Park are numerous preserved ruins of what was once a large and glorious city, and they rank among the most important of Thailand's ancient sites. The whole of the park has been landscaped, and is open 6am–6pm, and there is an admission fee.

Near Sukhothai are the remains of its satellite towns, Si Satchanalai and Kamphaeng Phet. Si Satchanalai is now un-inhabited, while Kamphaeng Phet is a thriving provincial centre. Both also have ruins dating from the Sukhothai era.

The town of *Phitsanulok* is about 55km (34 miles) to the east, and is used by some as a base for visiting Sukhothai. There are regular air services between Phitsanulok-Chiang Mai, and Phitsanulok-Bangkok, and the town has some good hotels. It also has an ancient temple with the Phra Buddha Chinarat, probably the most beautiful Buddha image. If you are travelling by road from Bangkok to Chiang Mai this is an good place for an overnight stop, as is Kamphaeng Phet, about 80km (50 miles) west of Sukhothai.

TOURS

Organised tours are available from Chiang Mai, and for information and reservations, enquire at your hotel information, or at the local branch of the Tourism Authority of Thailand, ph 235 334, 252 812. Here are a few examples.

City and Temples
A city tour with visits to the most interesting temples — Wat Phra Sing, Wat Chedi Luang, Wat Chiang Man, Wat Suan Dok, etc. — US$10–15.

Lamphun and Hariphunchai Temple
Wat Hariphunchai, one of the most sacred monuments in the

North, dates back to 1157. Also a visit to the village of Pasang —
US$14–17.

Handicraft Villages
See the home industries of lacquerware, weaving of Thai silk,
woodcarving, silverware and paper umbrellas — US$9–16.

Meos and Doi Suthep
Visit a Meo hilltribe village, Wat Doi Suthep and Phu-Ping Palace
— US$13–25.

Meo Mae Sa
Drive north to visit the Meo hilltribe village of Mae Sa. On the
way, visit the Ruckachati National Park and Mae Sa Waterfalls —
rates on application.

Elephants at Work
Visit an elephant working site and on the way back stop at the
Ruckachati National Park, the Ceramic Thai and Kilns of Celadon
at Mae Rim, or a large orchid farm — US$12–25.

Lisu Hilltribe Village
Visit an unspoilt Lisu hilltribe village and see the tribe of Tibeto
Burman stock. Of all the hill tribes found in Northern Thailand,
the costume worn by Lisu women is the most beautiful and
colourful — rates on application.

White Karen Hilltribe Village, Pasang and Lamphun
Visit a White Karen hilltribe village, Wat Phrabat Tak Pa with
footprints of the Lord Buddha, Pasang with its cotton looms, and
ancient Lamphun, with its temples, and Wat Chamathewi — rates
on application.

Chiang Rai/Chiang Saen/Golden Triangle
To Chiang Rai by road. Visit the archaeological remains at Chiang
Saen and Golden Triangle. On the way back visit E-Kaw and also
Meo hilltribe village. Lunch included — rates on application.

Suggested 6-Day Itinerary

Day One
Morning visit to Wat Phra Sing, Wat Chedi Luang, Wat Ku Tao.
After lunch, visit Wat Phra That Doi Suthep with its commanding

view of Chiang Mai. Late afternoon visit to Wat Suan Dok and/or Wat Umong.

Evening — Khantok dinner.

Day Two
Full-day trip to Mae Sa Valley to visit the Elephant Camp, orchid nurseries, waterfalls, hilltribe villages, and to enjoy an entertaining cultural show at little Chiang Mai.

Evening — leisure.

Day Three
Morning visit to Bo Sang Umbrella Village and Daytime Bazaar on Bo Sang — San Kamphaeng Road. After lunch, visit San Kampaeng Hot Springs.

Evening — leisure.

Day Four
Early morning departure for full-day trip to Doi Inthanon National Park. Visit Mae Kland, Wachirathan, Siriphum and Mae Pan waterfalls, Meo and Karen villages before reaching forested summit.

Evening — shopping in Chiang Mai's Night Bazaar.

Day Five
Full-day trip to Lamphun and Lampang. Visit Lamphun's Wat Phra That Hariphunchai and Lampang's Wat Lampang Luang. Lampang's major urban Burmese-style temples can be visited by horse-drawn carriages.

Evening — leisure.

Day Six
Early morning visit to Chiang Dao's Elephant Camp and Buddha-filled caves of Wat Tham Chiang Dao. From this point there is an option of travelling north to Fang and Tha Ton to travel by boat into Chiang Rai, or of returning to Chiang Mai.

SPORT AND RECREATION

Golf
Lanna Golf Course, Highway 107 (Chiang Mai-Mae Rim Road), Chiang Mai, ph 221 911. 7,174 yards, par 72. Open daily 6am–6pm.

Green fees — weekdays 150 baht; weekends 150 baht.
Caddy fee — 100 baht.
Clubs for hire — 200 baht.

Yim Cana, Chiang Mai-Lamphun Road, Chiang Mai. 9-hole course.

Green fees — weekdays 100 baht; weekends 100 baht.
Caddy fee — 50 baht.
Clubs for hire — 200 baht.

Girls from the Lisu Hilltribe in festival dress

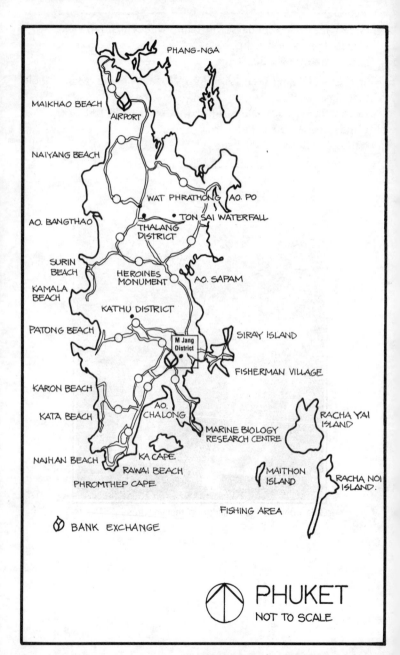

PHANG-NGA

MAIKHAO BEACH
AIRPORT

NAIYANG BEACH

WAT PHRATHONG   AO. PO

AO. BANGTHAO
• TON SAI WATERFALL
THALANG
DISTRICT

SURIN
BEACH
HEROINES
MONUMENT   AO. SAPAM

KAMALA
BEACH

KATHU DISTRICT

PATONG BEACH
M Jang
District   SIRAY ISLAND

KARON BEACH
FISHERMAN VILLAGE

KATA BEACH   AO.
CHALONG   RACHA YAI
ISLAND
MARINE BIOLOGY
RESEARCH CENTRE

NAIHAN BEACH   KA CAPE.   MAITHON
ISLAND   RACHA NOI
ISLAND.
RAWAI BEACH
PHROMTHEP CAPE.

FISHING AREA

◈ BANK EXCHANGE

△ PHUKET
NOT TO SCALE

PHUKET

Phuket is Thailand's largest island (approximately the size of Singapore) and nestles against the Indian Ocean coast 862 km (534 miles) south of Bangkok.

It derives its wealth from tin and rubber, has teeming marine life, and has enjoyed a rich and colourful history — the island's most famous landmark is the memorial statue of the heroines Thao Thep Kasattri and Thao Sisunthon, who rallied islanders in 1785 to repel invaders.

Phuket has magnificent coves and bays, powdery, palm-fringed white beaches, lushly forested mountains, waterfalls and parks. Delightful 1900 Indo/Portuguese and Chinese-influenced architecture creates an ambience suited to a relaxing holiday.

HOW TO GET THERE

By Air
Thai Airways has Boeing 737 flights at least 3 times daily from Bangkok, and the trip take one hour.

Thai Airways also has regular flights between Phuket and Penang, Kuala Lumpur and Singapore.

During its Bangkok-Singapore-Bangkok flights, Thai International lands at Phuket 4 times weekly.

By Bus
Government-operated buses and private air-conditioned tour coaches regularly make the 14 hour journey between Phuket and Bangkok. The Bus Terminal in Phuket is on Phang Nga Road, ph (076) 211 480.

There are no rail services to Phuket.

TOURIST INFORMATION
The local office of the Tourism Authority of Thailand is at 73–75 Phuket Road, Amphoe Muang, Phuket, ph (076) 212 213.

ACCOMMODATION

First-class hotels in the town offer complimentary transport to their own beach clubs. Economy-class hotels are also available within town. First-class resort hotels offer air-conditioned accommodation, as do many cabin and bungalow complexes on Phuket's most popular beaches. Other 'native-style' complexes, built of bamboo, rattan and Nipa palm thatch, dot the coastal hills and beaches to offer comfortable and relatively inexpensive accommodation.

The accommodation we have listed here is for a double room per night, and the prices, which should be taken as a guide only, are in bahts. The Telephone Area Code is 076.

First Class Hotels

Club Mediterranee, 7/3 mu 2 Tambon Karon, ph 214 830. The resort has everything expected of a Club Med resort. There are 300 guest rooms and prices range from 4,800–13,790 baht for full board.

Phuket Yacht Club Hotel & Beach Resort, 23/3 Viset Road, Nai Harn Beach, ph 214 020. Situated on a headland overlooking the beach at the south of Phuket Island, the resort has 100 guest rooms and 8 state-room suites. There are three restaurants, bar, coffee shop, health club, tennis courts, swimming pool and shopping arcade — 3,000 baht.

Superior Hotels

Cape Panwa Sheraton, 27 Mu 8, Sukdidej Capw Panwa, ph 391 123. A deluxe resort on the southern point of Phuket with all 142 rooms facing the ocean. Facilities include private beach, English Pub with entertainment, 2 restaurants, bar, coffee shop, tennis court, swimming pool, gymnasium and shopping arcade — 1,900 baht.

Coral Beach, 104 Mu 4, Patong Beach, ph 321 106. The hotel has superb views of the bay, and is only 10 minutes' walk from the central area of Patong Beach. There are 200 guest rooms, restaurant, bar, tennis courts, squash courts, swimming pool, disco and shopping arcade — 1,500–1,700 baht.

Diamond Cliff, Patong Beach, ph 321 195. Situated at the northern end of the beach, the hotel has 152 guest rooms, a restaurant, health club, swimming pool and tennis court — 2,460 baht.

Holiday Inn Phuket, 86/11 Taweewongse Road, Patong Beach, ph 321 020. Right on the beach, the hotel has 280 guest rooms, a choice of restaurants, lounges and bars, swimming pool, health club, tennis court and watersport equipment — 1,700 baht.

Karon Villa Phuket, 36/4 Karon Beach, ph 214 820. There are 325 guest rooms, restaurants, bar, coffee shop, health club, snooker club, tennis courts, swimming pool, nightclub and shopping arcade — 2,178–2,541 baht.

Le Meridien, 8/5 Mu 1, Tambon Karon, ph 321 480. Situated in a 14.5ha (36 acres) valley with a private 600m beach. All 470 guest rooms have sea views and there are restaurants, bar, 4 tennis courts, two squash courts, health club, swimming pools, archery range and games room — 2,450 baht.

Pearl Village, 42 Montri Road, ph 211 044. A modern resort with 250 guest rooms overlooking Naiyang Beach. Facilities include restaurant, bar, coffee shop, snooker club, swimming pool, 2 tennis courts, nightclub and shopping arcade — 840–1,100 baht.

Phuket Arcadia, Karon Beach, ph 214 841. Luxury accommodation in 255 guest rooms all will.sea views. Facilities include restaurants, bar, coffee shop, health club, snooker club, tennis court, putting green, swimming pool, nightclub and shopping arcade — 2,500 baht.

Standard Hotels

Pan Sea Phuket, 118 Mu 3, Tambon Choeng-Talay, Pan Sea Beach, ph 311 249 — 76 rooms — restaurant, bar, coffee shop, snooker club, swimming pool and shopping arcade — 2,200–2,700 baht.

Patong Merlin, 992 Mu 4, Patong Beach, ph 321 070 — 209 guest rooms — restaurant, bar, coffee shop, snooker club, swimming pool, videotheque, and shopping arcade — 1,600 baht.

Phuket Island Resort, 73/1 Rasada Road, Rawai Beach, ph 215 950 — 300 guest rooms — restaurant, bar, coffee shop, health club, snooker club, tennis court, swimming pool, disco and shopping arcade — 1,100–1,900 baht.

Tavorn Palm Beach — 128/10 Mu 3, Karon Beach, ph 214 835 — 210 guest rooms — restaurant, bar, coffee shop, health club, tennis court, swimming pool and shopping arcade — 2,480 baht.

Budget Hotels

City, 1-3-5 Krabi Road, ph 211 383 — 168 rooms — restaurant, bar, coffee shop, health club, snooker club, swimming pool, disco, shopping arcade — 700 baht.

Club Andaman Beach Resort, 77/1 Thaweewongse Road, ph 321 361 — 128 rooms — restaurant, bar, coffee shop, health club, swimming pool and shopping arcade — 750 baht.

Holiday Resort, Patong Beach, Kathu, ph 321 101 — 105 guest rooms — restaurant, bar, coffee shop, health club, swimming pool, videotheque — 860 baht.

Pearl, 42 Montri Road, ph 211 044 — 250 guest rooms — restaurant, bar, coffee shop, snooker club, swimming pool, nightclub and shopping arcade — 720–840 baht.

Phuket Merlin, 158/1 Jawaaj Road, ph 212 866 — 180 rooms — restaurant, bar, coffee shop, health club, swimming pool, disco, shopping arcade — 880–1,060 baht.

LOCAL TRANSPORT

Motorcycles, jeeps and cars may be rented to explore Phuket's many lovely beaches.

Taxis can be hired through your hotel, or in front of the Thavom Hotel. The rates are set according to the time hired and distance travelled, and there is a minimum rate.

There are also buses and share-taxis available, which have established routes — enquire at your hotel as to the routes and prices.

EATING OUT

Standard western fare is found in major hotels and coffee shops. Thai, Chinese and Islamic food is available islandwide. Phuket's seafood, probably Thailand's most delicious, is prepared in a variety of succulent styles. Southern Thai food can be spicy hot but local specialities, such as spicy mango salads, are well worth sampling. Tropical fruits abound, particularly local pineapples and coconuts.

The standard of food in the hotels and resorts is excellent, but if you would like a change here are a few suggestions:

Tun Ka Cafe, Rang Hill, with a great view of the town of
  Phuket.
Chao Fah, on Chao Fah Road.
Tai Fah, opposite the Pearl Theatre.
Lai-an, 58 Rasda Road.
Jack and Joy, Pang Nga Road.
There are many small restaurants outside the main tourist areas,
and these are worth trying as they are usually cheaper, and just as
hygienic as the larger establishments.

ENTERTAINMENT

Phuket's nightlife is sedate compared with Bangkok, Pattaya or
Hat Yai, and is concentrated largely in the town centre and Patong
Beach.

SHOPPING

The local gift shops customarily stock popular handicrafts from all
over Thailand, southern batiks and local products, such as handcrafted coral and shell ornaments, seashells and cultured pearls.

SIGHTSEEING

Phuket Town

The compact provincial capital serves mainly as a dormitory and
shopping centre. Splendid colonial-style residences built by late
19th century tin and rubber barons, and shops with shaded
walkways from the same period create a distinctive character.

  Rang Hill offers a pleasant view of town and has a Fitness Park,
a series of hillside sculptural tableaux which enhance keep-fit
calisthenics.

  Southern Thailand's largest Crocodile Farm, containing
aquariums featuring colourful coral fish found in the coastal waters,
and hundreds of marine, freshwater and estuarine crocodiles and
alligators, lies just outside town.

  Several companies arrange local tours, beach trips, visits to
cultured pearl farms, island cruises and exploration, and 2–5 day
scuba-diving 'seafaris'.

Island Attractions

Phuket's Indian Ocean coastline has the best beaches, while the eastern coastline overlooks some 30 lesser islands occupying largely tranquil seas. The islands vary greatly in size, some are large enough to sustain fishing communities, coconut plantations, deer and wild boar. Others are little larger than massive rocks. Others again resemble fortresses, and are riddled with caves containing the birds' nests prized by gourmets.

Counter-clockwise from Phuket's northern tip, the island's major beaches, temples and botanical parks are as follows:

Mai Khao Beach, 34 km (21 miles) from town, is Phuket's longest beach. Between November and February each year, gigantic sea turtles struggle ashore to lay their eggs.

Nai Yang Beach, 30 km (19 miles) from town to the south, forms part of a National Park and is peaceful, excellent for swimming and relaxation.

Wat Ohra Thong, inland from Nai Yang Beach, is where a famous partially-buried Buddha is enshrined.

Ton Sai Waterfall Forest Park and *Khao Phra Thaeo Wildlife Park* are further east, 20 km (12 miles) from town. There are innumerable birds, wild boars and monkeys in the parks, and the cascades offer refreshing coolness.

Further south, *Pansea Bay, Surin Beach,* 24 km (15 miles) from town, *Sing Cape* and *Kamala Beach* unfold in rapid succession. A public 9-hole golf course fronts Surin Beach where swimming is not recommended due to powerful surf and a treacherous undertow. The northern end of Kamala Beach, however, is suitable for swimming.

Patong Beach, 20 km (12 miles) from town, is Phuket's most developed beach. Cabin and bungalow complexes, hotels, bars, nightclubs, discotheques, shops and restaurants front the crescent bay. Windsurfing, snorkelling, sailing, sunbathing and swimming are the major activities.

Karon, 20 km (12 miles), and *Kata,* 17 km (11 miles) from town, are the next major beaches. Both are long, and suitable for swimming, windsurfing, sailing, snorkelling and sunbathing. Kata is partially fronted by the Club Mediteranee complex.

Nai Han Beach, 18 km (11 miles) from town, fronts a shallow lagoon between steep headlands. Swimming, windsurfing, sailing, sunbathing and snorkelling are popular activities.

Promthep Cape, near Nai Han Beach, marks Phuket's southernmost point and is the place from which to view spectacular sunsets.

Rawai Beach, 17 km (11, miles) from the town to the east of Promthep Cape, hosts Phuket's best known 'sea gypsies' (the shell fishermen of the village of Moken). Several offshore islands have gleaming white beaches and great underwater scenery that attracts dedicated scuba-divers.

Chalong Bay, 11 km (7 miles) from town, to the north-east, extends in a broad sweep. A few kilometres inland, Wat Chalong has statues of Luang Pho Chaem and Luang Pho Chuang, Phuket's most revered monks.

Phuket's Aquarium and a *Marine Biolgical Research Centre* are on the southernmost tip of Phanwa Cape, 10 km (6 miles) from town. The aquarium has several hundred exotic, grotesque and flamboyantly colourful marine species.

OUTLYING ATTRACTIONS

Phuket is a convenient place from which to visit attractions in the neighbouring provinces of Phang Nga and Krabi.

Phang Nga's major attraction is the eeerily beautiful Phang Nga Bay which has been featured in several Thai and international movies, most notably the James Bond adventure "The Man With The Golden Gun".

Green limesone islands, honeycombed with caves and grottoes, soar perpendicularly some 300 m (980 ft), from almost perpetually calm waters. The bay's many moods range from early morning mists to colourful sunsets.

Few islands are inhabited and except for the occasional fishing village, the bay is largely untouched by human hand.

Major attractions include Kiang Mount, Panyi Isle, Nom Sao Isle, Thalu Isle, Kho Phing Kan Isle (James Bond Island), Tapu Mount, Ma Chu Mount and Lot Cave.

Krabi's major attractions are the beautiful Phi Phi islands — Phi Phi Don and Phi Phi Le — which can be visited either from

Phuket or Krabi's provincial capital in a boat ride lasting about 3 hours. The boat trip from Krabi is less expensive and slightly shorter.

Phi Phi Don is gently undulating with many beautiful beaches and viewpoints. Phi Phi Le is mainly rocky with towering cliffs. Underwater scenery around this island is remarkably beautiful, with crystal clear waters and a relatively shallow seabed offering unique sights of coral reefs and marine life.

The islands are best visited Nov–Dec, when seas are calm and at their clearest.

Other Krabi attractions, less than 30 minutes from the capital, are the beautiful Nopparat Beach and Susan Hoi, a 75-million-year-old shell cemetery where fossilised shells form tiered, concrete-like slabs. Susan Hoi is one of only three such shell cemeteries in the world.

Suggested 8-Day Itinerary

Day One
Morning exploration of Phuket town, including a visit to Crocodile Farm. Afternoon visit to Phuket's Aquarium, Wat Chalong, Karon, Kata and Rawai Beaches before viewing the sunset from Promthep Cape.

Evening — leisure/dinner on Rang Hill.

Day Two
Morning check-in to Patong Beach hotel/cabin/bungalow. Afternoon relaxation/water sports; and exploration of scenic coastal road which connects Patong with secluded coves, Kamala Beach, Sing Cape, Surin Beach and Pansea Bay.

Evening — leisure/Patong nightlife.

Day Three
Full day of relaxation at Patong; sunbathing/swimming/windsurfing/fishing/snorkelling/sailing, etc.

Evening — leisure/Patong nightlife.

Day Four
Morning departure by road for Phang Nga, visiting en route Ton Sai Waterfall Forest Park, and Khao Phra Thaeo Wildlife Park, and the peaceful Nai Yang Beach.

Evening — overnight stay at Phang Nga's resort hotel.

Fishing Fleet in Songkhla

Samui Island beach scene

Day Five
Early-morning departure for boat excursion to Phang Nga Bay, visiting major attractions such as Khian Mount, Panyi's stilted fishing village, James Bond Island and Tapu Mount. Mid-afternoon return to Phuket to check-in to hotel/cabin/bungalow in town, botanical garden or beach of preference.

Day Six
Full day of relaxation devoted to the pleasures of sun, sand 'n' sea.
   Evening — leisure.

Day Seven
Morning departure for 3-hour boat trip to Krabi's Phi Phi islands. Explore Phi Phi Don, swim, sunbathe, snorkel, etc. Overnight stay at Phi Phi Don which has comfortable cabin accommodation with restaurant facilities.

Day Eight
Morning exploration of Phi Phi Le, snorkelling, swimming, etc. before return journey to Phuket where visitors may extend their island sojourn or travel onwards to other destinations.

DIVING
There are half day tours available to the west coast where a short trip by motor boat takes you to the coral reefs which are typical of this area, with a great variety of soft sites offering relaxed diving and good close-up photo opportunities with dives up to 35 m.

By far the most popular tours, however, are the full day trips to the islands lying off Phuket's south and eastern coasts. These islands include Ko Racha, Shark Point, Ko Dok Mai and Ko Phi Phi.

Ko Racha lies to the south of Phuket some 2 hours away by motor boat. The Racha Islands have dives of up to 30 m and visibility from 20 to 40 m. In addition there are huge rock formations, sloping coral reefs and steep drop offs. From January to March Manta Rays and Whale Sharks can occasionally be seen here in additional to the many varieties of tropical marine life.

Shark Point and Ko Dok Mai are approximately 1.5 hours by motor boat to the east of Phuket and are without doubt two of the most popular dive sites. Shark Point, a submerged reef, is a favourite haunt of leopard sharks and sting rays. It is an underwater photographers' dream come true. The visibility at Shark Point is between 10 and 22 m with dives up to 25 m. The Island of Ko Dok Mai offers dives of up to 30 m with visibility of 10–25 m.

Ko Phi Phi has been voted one of the most beautiful islands in the world, and is also an excellent dive destination. In addition to the vast array of hard and soft corals, there are cave dives and many impressive wall dives. There is an abundant marine life, including white tip sharks, sting rays and moray eels. Phi Phi is some 40 km (25 miles) south-east of Phuket and is about 2 hours away by motor boat. The dives are from 10–30 m with visibility 15–25 m.

Ko Similan or Similan Islands are a group of nine virtually uninhabited tropic islands approximately 80 km (50 miles) north-west of Phuket Island. They are a Marine National Park and increasing efforts are being made to keep the islands in their present condition. The diving ranges from coral gardens to adventurous drift diving in strong current conditions. A selection of the diving available is as follows.

Ko Huyong, the southern most island of the group offers a magnificent coral garden in 20–40 m of water. The garden consists of many varieties of soft and hard corals and abounds with small coral fish. This site frequently has over 30 m visibility, only slight currents, and is a very safe and enjoyable dive.

An extensive reef runs off another of the southern islands and provides at least 4 different dive sites. One bottoms out at 25 m and has many large rocks which provide a most interesting contour, with many large schools of fish. Another part of the reef provides an excellent 20 m dive and has a lot of small lava type rocks which provide a home for anemones, hydroids and soft corals as well as moray eels and red grouper. The visibility is seldom less than 30 m and frequently more. There is often a strong current here which makes these excellent drift dives.

The central island of the group, Ko Miang, is the only island which is inhabited. There is also a number of excellent dive sites around this and the small adjoining island, including one which features huge boulders leaning together forming many interesting tunnels and small caverns. This dive often has a strong surge which attracts a large variety of marine life. Small white tip sharks, rays, snapper and turtle are just a few of the varieties. An excellent night dive site is just around the corner, close to a safe overnight anchorage and a white sanded beach. This dive site is a coral drop off and depths range from 10–20 m with little current present making it ideal for a safe night dive.

Hin Pousar or Elephant Rock is one of the best known dive locations and provides at least 3 more excellent sites. There are again many big holes and caverns formed by the unusual rock formations, and the encrustations, anemones and coral provide a kaleidoscope of reds, yellow, blues and browns. Frequently large rays, tuna, or barracuda can be seen.

Further to the north near the top of Ko Similan lies an offshore reef which comes up to within 8 m of the surface and drops off to over 35 m. More tunnels, hollows and chimneys provide a site that never fails to impress even the most experienced diver. Seldom is the visibility at any of these sites less than 25m and usually much more.

Dive Centres/Schools

Fantasea Divers, Patong Beach, (P.O. Box 74, Phuket), ph 321 309. Contact Maarten Brusselers.

Marina Sports, Marina Cottage, Kata Karon Beach, ph 212 901–4 ext. Marina, (P.O. Box 143, Phuket). Contact Frank Lamine.

Ocean Divers, Patong Beach Hotel, ph 321 166. Contact Prasert Banmuang.

Phuket Aquatic Safari, 62/9 Rasada Centre, Rasada Road, ph 216 562. Contact Peter Lee.

Phuket Divers, 7/70 Phunphon Road, ph 215 738. Contact Verrasak Eamsakuirat.

Phuket Int. Diving Centre, Coral Beach Hotel, ph 321 106–15. Contact Eric Dohion. OR Le Meridien Hotel, ph 321 480–5. Contact Guy (Charlie) Lidureau.

Poseidon Memrod Club, Phuket Island Resort, ph 215 950–5. Contact Klaus Orlik.

Santana, Patong Beach, (P.O. Box 79, Phuket), ph 321 360, OR Kata Beach, ph 292 901–4. Contact Horst Hinrishs, Dieter Eichier.

Siam Diving Centre, Kata Karon Beach, (P.O. Box 244, Phuket), ph 212 901–4 ext. 014. Contact Matthew Hedrick.

South East Asia, 89/71 Thawiwong Road, Patong Beach, (P.O. Box 199, Phuket), ph 321 292. Contact Dave Owen.

Rates for the various tours obviously vary according to the dive centre responsible for the organisation of the trip. But as a guide, a typical half day diving trip to Phuket's west coast costs approximately 900 baht per person, which includes rental of complete equipment.

- a full day diving trip to the west coast, with complete equipment — 1,250 baht.
- a tour to Ko Phi Phi, with full equipment — 2,250 baht per day.
- five day/six night tour to the Similan Islands, with full equipment and meals — 10,500 — 12,500 baht, according to the season.

GOLF
The Phuket Golf and Country Club is the first major 18-hole course on the island. The 6,393 yards, par 72 course is located on the main road between Phuket town and the beach of Patong, ph 213 388.

SONGKHLA AND HAT YAI

Southern Thailand's Songkhla province is richly endowed with natural resources, fine beaches, waterfalls and scenic lakes, yet its two major cities, Songkhla, the provincial capital and Hat Yai, separated by a mere 30 minute road journey, are a world apart in terms of attractions, facilities, size and character.

Songkhla, 974 km (604 miles) from Bangkok, was a medieval pirate stronghold, and is now a sleepy, historic town with a thriving fishing community, and a fine beach facing the Thai Gulf. It was here that the Cambodian 'boat people' arrived in the late 1970s, and the refugee camp on the beach is a deterrent to a lot of visitors.

Hat Yai, 947 km (587 miles) from Bangkok, is a modern, inland city, and the major gateway to southern Thailand. It is the principal southern commercial, communications and entertainment area.

A study in contrasts, Songkhla province boasts several authentic tourism attractions, and Hat Yai makes an excellent base for exploring Thailand's southernmost destinations.

HOW TO GET THERE

By Air
Thai Airways has at least one flight a day from Bangkok to Hat Yai, and flight time is 1 hour 15 minutes by direct flights.

There are also regular connections with Hat Yai and Butterworth/Penang, Kuala Lumpur and Singapore.

By Rail
Daily rail services are available from Bangkok to Hat Yai, and there are regular connections with Butterworth/Penang, Kuala Lumpur and Singapore. The train trip from Bangkok to Hat Yai takes 17 hours.

By Bus
Daily bus services are available from Bangkok, and regular services from Malaysia and Singapore. Hat Yai is 3 hours by air-conditioned

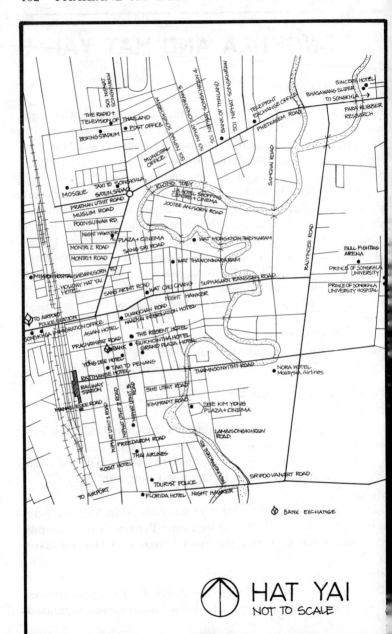

HAT YAI
NOT TO SCALE

coach from Penang, 12 hours from Kuala Lumpur, 19 hours from Singapore, and 15 hours from Bangkok.

There are no direct rail or air services to Songkhla.

TOURIST INFORMATION
The Hat Yai office of the Tourism Authority of Thailand is at 1/1 Soi 2 Niphat Uthit 3 Road, ph (074) 243 747, 245 986.

ACCOMMODATION
Hat Yai boasts several first-class air-conditioned hotels with international facilities and innumerable economy-class hotels, inns and guest houses.

Songkhla's accommodation is less luxurious and varied, its major hotel is a beachside complex facing Songkhla's famous mermaid statue on the Samila Beach headland.

The accommodation we have listed here is for a double room per night. The prices are in bahts, and should be used as a guide only. The Telephone Area Code is 074.

HAT YAI
Superior Hotels
JB Hat Yai, 99 Jootee Anusorn Road, ph 234 300 — 208 guest rooms — restaurant, bar, coffee shop, swimming pool, health club, disco and shopping arcade — 1,210 baht.

Lee Gardens, 1 Lee Phattana Road, ph 234 420 — 122 guest rooms — restaurant and videotheque — 835 baht.

Standard Hotels
Asian Hat Yai, 55 Niphat-Uthit 3 Road, ph 245 455 — 104 guest rooms — restaurant, bar, coffee shop, videotheque — 420–450 baht.

Emperor, 1 Tanrattanakon Road, ph 245 166 — 108 guest rooms — restaurant, bar, coffee shop, disco — 425 baht.

Hat Yai Inter, 42-44 Niphat Uthit 3 Road, ph 244 744 — 210 guest rooms — restaurant — 637 baht.

Montein, 120-124 Niphat Uthit Road, ph 245 399 — 180 guest rooms — restaurant — 532 baht.

New World, 144-150 Niphat Uthit 2 Road, ph 246 993 — 133 guest rooms — restaurant, swimming pool, videotheque — 726 baht.

Nora, 216 Thammanoonvithi Road, ph 244 944 — 170 guest rooms — restaurant, swimming pool, videotheque — 515 baht.

Sukhontha, 26 Sanehanusorn Road, ph 243 999 — 205 guest rooms — restaurant and swimming pool — 545 baht.

Budget Hotels
Ambassador, 23 Sriphadung-Phakdi Road, ph 234 410 — 170 guest rooms — coffee shop, videotheque — 370 baht.

City, Saiburi Road, ph 312 628 — 67 guest rooms — restaurant, videotheque — 350 baht.

Kings, 126 Niphat-Uthit Road, ph 234 966 — 88 guest rooms — restaurant, coffee shop — 320 baht.

Kosit, 199 Niphat-Uthit 2 Road, ph 235 710 — 182 guest rooms — restaurant, bar, coffee shop, disco — 417 baht.

SONGKHLA
Samila Beach, 1/11 Ratchadamnoen Road, ph 311 310 — 70 guest rooms and 5 bungalows — restaurant, coffee shop, golf course, swimming pool — 700 baht.

LOCAL TRANSPORT
There is a local bus service, and cars may be hired through the hotels.

EATING OUT AND ENTERTAINMENT
If Songkhla is most attractive by day, Hat Yai is most attractive by night. Other than a 40 ha (100 acre) municipal park where southern cultural performances are regularly staged, and a crocodile farm and zoo on Ratchawithi Road, Hat Yai's major attraction is its vibrant nightlife which draws innumerable pleasure-seekers, particularly from Malaysia and Singapore.

Numerous first-class Chinese, Thai, Japanese, Muslim and seafood restaurants provide excellent cuisine, while international fare is enjoyed in several coffee shops and leading hotels.

The nightlife revolves largely around nightclubs, coffee shops, bars, bowling alleys, massage parlours, video houses, cinemas and discotheques.

SHOPPING

Hat Yai offers particularly good buys in Thai handicrafts, ready-made leisurewear and sportswear, preserved Thai fruits and seafood delicacies, as well as imported foodstuffs from all over South-East Asia and China.

The main shopping areas are around the Niphat Uthit 2 and 3 Roads and the Plaza Market.

Songkhla's major shops selling local products, including the native cotton product Pha Ko Yo, dried shrimps, cashew nuts, crisp fish and shrimp crackers, and the leather sheets for shadow-play puppets, are in the Nakhon Nai Road area.

SIGHTSEEING

SONGKHLA

Samila Beach
The beach is the major attraction in Songkhla. It faces the small Cat and Mouse Islands, and extends some 3 km southwards to Khao Seng headland which shelters a Muslim fishing village. The Samila headland features a mermaid statue, fronting a beachside hotel with a 9-hole golf course to the south, and beachside seafood restaurants to the north.

Khao Noi
This is a low hill behind the hotel, which overlooks Samila Beach and Songkhla's northern shore. It has a small topiary garden.

Museum
On Rongmuang Road there is a 19th century Chinese mansion which houses the local branch of the National Museum.

Wat Matchimawat
On Saiburi Road, this temple is 400 years old, and is the largest temple in Songkhla. It contains a small museum.

Wat Chaimongkon
This temple is near Songkhla's former railway station.

Pak Mae Nam Lai Soet Fort
On Lai Soet Road, the fort dates from the early 1800s when modern' Songkhla was built.

Sinakarinwirot University
The University's Institute for Southern Thai Studies is a few kilometres from town on Route 407, which connects Songkhla and Hat Yai. The Institute has a fine collection of southern handicrafts, religious manuscripts, antiques and archaeological finds.

NEIGHBOURING ATTRACTIONS

Phatthalung
The town is 115 km (71 miles) from Hat Yai. Near here, on the northern end of the Songkhla Great Lake, the lotus-bordered Thale Noi Nok Nam bird sanctuary is home to some 150 different species.

Trang
65 km (40 miles) further west, Trang is in the mountainous Khao Chong Nature Reserve, which contains one of southern Thailand's most scenic waterfalls.

Pattani
To the south, 109 km (68 miles) from Hat Yai, Pattani has Thailand's most beautiful mosque, the famous Wat Chang Hai. The sweeping Panare Beach is nearby. It is home to local fishermen who are known for their hundreds of hand-painted Kolae boats.

Narathiwat
100 km (62 miles) further south, Narathiwat is noted for its Pa Cho Waterfall. Nearby is a massive seated golden Buddha at Wat Khao Kung, and the border town of Sungei Golok noted for its seedy nightlife.

OUTLYING ATTRACTIONS

Great Songkhla Lake
Known locally as Thale Sap, this is Songkhla's major provincial attraction. It extends some 80 km (50 miles) north from Songkhla's fishing port, and is some 20 km (12 miles) at its widest point. The lake is dotted with small islands and hosts the 520 km^2 (201 sq

miles) Khu Khut Waterfowl Park, Asia's largest, which supports 140 species numbering tens of thousands of birds.

Khu Khut is reached by crossing the lake's estuarine entrance at Songkhla and proceeding northwards along Route 4083. At Km. 33, a left turn leads to Khu Khut village where you can hire boats to explore the Waterfowl Park. Khu Khut is best visited in the early morning or late afternoon when the birds are more active.

Wat Pakho
Situated 10 km (6 miles) north of Khu Khu is the ancient Wat Pakho, former residence of southern Thailand's most revered abbot, the late Luang Pho Thuat.

A popular legend claims the abbot was kidnapped by pirates while crossing the lake. A violent storm arose and the boat carrying the abbot and his captors drifted for several days. Lacking food and water, everyone faced starvation. Then the abbot placed his foot in the lake's salt water, whereupon it became drinkable. The pirates were so grateful they returned the abbot safely to shore.

Ton Nga Chang (Elephant Tusk) Waterfall
This well-known waterfall lies some 26 km (16 miles) west of Hat Yai in the Rattaphum district along Highway No. 4, and at the end of a turning from Hu Rae village.

The seven-tiered waterfall cascades down a steep cliff in two separate columns resembling elephant tusks. The fall's third level is particularly quiet and beautiful, and affords a very good view of surrounding countryside. It is a very difficult climb and should not be attempted by the aged.

Boriphat Waterfall
This is another waterfall worth visiting in the Rattaphum district, about 40 km (25 miles) from Hat Yai.

Satun
Satun, 102 km (63 miles) south-west of Hat Yai, is the capital of a province whose main attraction is the sprawling Tarutao Marine National Park.

Tarutao Marine National Park
Situated 30 km (19 miles) off the coast near the Thai-Malaysian Indian Ocean maritime border. The 51 island cluster covers a total

sea and land area of about 1,400 km² (540 sq miles). It offers simple bungalow accommodation and camping facilities, and some of South-East Asia's best scuba-diving. For the enthusiast there are dolphins, whales, smaller sharks, sea turtles, rockfish, colourful coral fish and soft coral.

Weekend trips originating in Hat Yai make regular departures from Pak Bara port in Satun's Langu distrist to Tarutao between the non-monsoon months of December and April.

Suggested 7-Day Itinerary

Day One
Check into Hat Yai hotel/inn/guest house. Explore city, shopping attractions, and enjoy afternoon performance in Southern Culture Village. (Check with hotel for performance times).

Evening — leisure/shopping/nightlife.

Day Two
Mid-morning check-out and depart for Songkhla. Visit Southern Institute for Thai Studies before checking in to a beachside hotel. Afternoon of relaxation on Samila Beach. Visit to Kao Seng and Muslim fishing village optional.

Evening — leisure/seafood dinner.

Day Three
Morning visit to National Museum and Wat Matchimawat. Early afternoon departure for Wat Pakho, mid- and late-afternoon excursion through Khu Khut Waterfowl Park which is known for its spectacular sunsets.

Evening — leisure/overnight stay in Songkhla.

Day Four
Morning departure for Hat Yai. Check-in to hotel/inn/guest house and spend remainder of day visiting Boriphat and Ton Nga Chang waterfalls.

Evening — leisure/shopping/nightlife.

Day Five
Between December and April, join excursion tour to Tarutao, either from Hat Yai or Pak Bara port in Satun's Langu district. Overnight stay at Tarutao's Phante Bay Park Headquarters.

Day Six
Excursion boats customarily visit the Adang-Rawi island cluster 40 km (25 miles) west of Tarutao island. Adang island offers simple accommodation. Visit Rawi and Hin Ngam islands where waters are excellent for snorkelling. Overnight stay on Adang.

Day Seven
Return to Pak Bara and Hat Yai, where travellers have the option of extending their Hat Yai/Songkhla sojourn, visiting further neighbouring destinations, or taking afternoon flights to Phuket or Bangkok.

GOLF

Ton Yai Golf Course (Songkhla)
Nine relatively easy holes on well maintained greens and fairways. Address is c/- Samila Hotel, Songkhla, ph 311 310.
   Green fees — weekdays 100 baht; weekends 100 baht.
   Caddy fee — 100 baht.

Kho Hong Golf Course (Hat Yai)
9-Hole course with several interesting holes and well-kept greens, ph 243 605.
   Green fees — weekdays 100 baht; weekends 150 baht.
   Caddy fee — 50 baht.

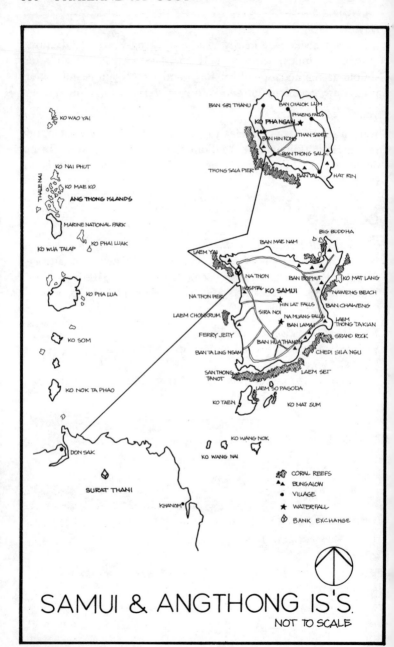

SAMUI & ANGTHONG IS'S.
NOT TO SCALE

SURAT THANI

Surat Thani is southern Thailand's largest province — about 12,800 km² (4,941 sq miles) — and has an extensive coastline lapped by limpid Gulf waters.

Besides beautiful beaches, Surat Thani boasts some of Thailand's most attractive tropical islands, namely the Penang-sized Ko Samui, Thailand's third largest island, which includes the stunning 250 km² (97 sq miles) Angthong (Golden Bowl) Marine National Park.

Surat Thani once formed part, and may have been the centre, of the Mahayana Buddhist Srivichaya empire which, steeped in legend and mystery, dominated the Malay peninsula and most of Java about 1,500 years ago. Archaeological finds in the Chaiya district clearly indicate the former empire's splendour.

Surat Thani's present provincial capital, 630 km (391 miles) south of Bangkok by road, is a thriving commercial, entertainment and communications centre, and is fast becoming a popular destination.

HOW TO GET THERE

By Air
Thai Airways have at least one flight a day from Bangkok to Surat Thani. Flying time is one hour. Air schedules are available from Thai Airways, Bangkok, ph 282 2764.

By Rail
There are daily rail services between Bangkok and Surat Thani. The trip takes 13 hours, so the most convenient is an overnight train. Rail schedules can be obtained from Bangkok's Hualamphong Station, ph 223 7461.

By Bus
Air-conditioned and regular coaches leave Bangkok's Southern Bus Terminal on Charansanitwong Road, ph 414 4978–9 (air) and 411 0511 (regular) throughout the day.

TOURIST INFORMATION

The local office of the Tourism Authority of Thailand is in the Sala Prachakhom Building, Na Muang Road, Amphoe Muang, ph (077) 282 828, 281 828.

ACCOMMODATION

First-class and economy-class hotels are found in Surat Thani. Accommodation in Ko Samut is confined largely to air-conditioned and non air-conditioned, moderately priced beachside bungalows. A listing of accommodation currently available may be obtained from the local Tourist Information Office.

The selection of accommodation listed below is in bahts for a double room per night, and should be used as a guide only. The Telephone Area Code is 077.

Surat Thani

Siam Thani, 180 Surat Phunphin Road, ph 273 081 — 170 guest rooms — bar, coffee shop, swimming pool, tennis court, disco, shopping arcade — 360–390 baht.

Siam Thara, 1/144 Donnok Road, ph 273 740 — 172 guest rooms — coffee shop — 252–600 baht.

Thanawat, Chon Kasem Road, ph 272 473 — 50 guest rooms — restaurant, disco — 150–250 baht.

Wang Tai, 1 Talad Mai Road, ph 273 410 — 238 guest rooms — restaurant, bar, coffee shop, swimming pool, golf course, disco and shopping arcade — 650–750 baht.

Samui Island

Coral Bay Resort, 9 Mu 2, Tambon Bo-Phut, ph 272 222 — 36 guest rooms — restaurant, tennis court, swimming pool, video-theque, shopping arcade — 800–900 baht.

Chao Koh Bungalow, 29/4 Mu 3 Tambon Ang Thong, ph 421 214 — 18 rooms — restaurant — 250 baht.

Nara Lodge, 80-81 Mu 4 Big Buddha Beach, ph 421 364 — 45 guest rooms — restaurant, bar, coffee shop, tennis court, swimming pool, shopping arcade — 600–800 baht.

Sand Sea Resort, Hat Lamai, Ko Samui, ph 421 415 — 20 guest rooms — restaurant, bar, swimming pool — 500 baht.

Low tide, Surat Thani

Long beach, Phi Phi Islands

Ferry in Ko Samui

The Village, 101 Mu 3, Chaweng Beach, ph 421 382 — 19 guest rooms — restaurant, bar — 1,000 baht.

LOCAL TRANSPORT
Ko Samui can be reached by ferry, speedboat and car ferry from Ban Don and Don Sak. Current fares and timetables are available from Surat Thani's Tourism Authority of Thailand office.

Bangkok Airways, ph 253 4014–5 Bangkok, have regular air services between Bangkok and Ko Samui.

EATING OUT
The entertainment is centred around the hotels, which have excellent dining rooms, and some have cocktail bars and discotheques.

SIGHTSEEING
Visitors interested in Buddhism and antiquity will want to visit Wat Suan Mokkhaphalaram, 25 km (15 miles) north of Surat Thani's airport on Route 41, and Chaiya's Phra Boromathat Chaiya.

Wat Suan Mokkhaphalaram
Better known as Suan Mok, this is an unusual 61 ha (150 acre) forest temple whose monastic community follows the simple regimen of the Buddha's earliest disciples. Suan Mok is devoid of extravagant ceremonial chapels with multi-tiered roofs. Sculpture workshops dot the forested enclave, and physical labour is an essential part of the community's lifestyle.

Suan Mok's founder and abbot, Bhikkhu Buddhadhasa, is highly respected in Thailand, and internationally, and his 'back-to-basics' approach attracts Buddhist monks and lay meditators from Europe, North and South America, Australia and Japan.

A favourite sight for casual visitors is the Spiritual Theatre which Buddhadhasa describes as a "pictorial interpretation of Karma". The building features an eclectic mixture of Thai, Egyptian, Chinese, Indian, Japanese, Tibetan and European-style murals and sculpture.

Phra Boromathat Chaiya
It is one of Buddhism's revered shrines, and is near the Chaiya

railway station. The elaborately restored pagoda is over 1,200 years old. It contains Buddha relics, and is a direct link with the Srivichaya empire. A small museum nearby houses relics from the vicinity.

Phumriang Village
6 km (4 miles) east of Chaiya, Phumriang is an arts and crafts centre, and is well known for its silk cloth and jute hats.

Ko Samui
Surat Thani's major tourist attraction, Ko Samui is a 247 km² (95 sq mile) island 268 nautical miles south of Bangkok. It has numerous beaches and bays, is almost literally covered in coconuts (some 2 million are shipped monthly to Bangkok!) and forested hills. It is fast becoming a resort of international stature.

Samui's best beaches are on the northern and eastern coasts, the most popular being Chaweng and Lamai.

Besides beaches, other island attractions include the Hin Lat and Na Muang waterfalls; the phallic rock formations at the southern end of Lamai Bay; a massive seated Buddha image on Pan isle in Pla Laem Bay; and Na Thon, the island's major seafront settlement where shops, restaurants, tour agencies and hotels are located.

Angthong Marine National Park comprises some 40 islands north-west of Ko Samui and covers about 250 km² (97 sq miles).

Major islands in the park (largely towering, verdant rock masses encircled by clear seas), include Mae Ko, Sam Sao with a coral reef and huge rock arch, and Phai Luak.

Ko Pha Ngan, the large island 60 minutes directly north of Ko Samui, has the Than Sadet waterfall and an extensive coral reef, while even further north, the remote Ko Tao shelters some of the Gulf's best, and largely unexplored scuba-diving waters.

OUTLYING ATTRACTIONS
Surat Thani is a convenient base for visiting neighbouring southern provinces.

Chumphon
To the north of Surat Thani, and 460 km (285 miles) from

Bangkok, Chumphon has very good beaches, birds' nest islands and excellent scuba-diving waters.

Ranong
Ranong is to the north-west and is 564 km (350 miles) from Bangkok. Here we find the Chansom Thara Hot Spa Health Resort, which draws water from Thailand's only Geo-Thermal Mineral Water Spring, and offers a 'get-fit' holiday, fishing and island cruises in the Indian Ocean.

Nakhon Si Thammarat
This province, 784 km (486 miles) from Bangkok, is home to one of Thailand's oldest temples, Wat Phra Maha That, and centre of southern Thai handicrafts such as neilloware, Yan Liphao basketry, leather shadow-play figures and Thai silk brocades.

Suggested 6-Day Itinerary

Day One
Morning flight from Bangkok. Mid-morning, early-afternoon visits to Suan Mok and Phra Boromathat Chaiya. Overnight stay in Surat Thani.

Day Two
Morning departure from Don Sak or Ban Don to Ko Samui. Afternoon exploration of island by rented motorcycle or jeep to locate preferred beach and accommodation. Overnight stay on Ko Samui.

Day Three
Full day of relaxation at beach of preference, swimming, wind-surfing, sailing, snorkelling, etc. Overnight stay on Ko Samui.

Day Four
Detailed island exploration, visiting Hin Lat and Na Muang waterfalls, seated Buddha image on Fan isle, phallic rock formations at Lamai Bay, etc. Overnight stay.

Day Five
Full-day excursion to Angthong Marine National Park, visiting Mae ko's Tale Nai and Wua Talap. Option of overnight stay, or return to Ko Samui.

Day Six
After return to Ko Samui, or morning of relaxation, return by ferry or speedboat to Don Sak or Ban Don for overnight stay in Surat Thani before returning to Bangkok; or continuing southern exploration.

Hua Hin's "Klai Kangwon" palace

CHA AM AND HUA HIN

Cha Am, 173 km (107 miles) south-west of Bangkok, and Hua Hin, 240 km (149 miles) south-west of Bangkok, are coastal towns on the 'sunrise' side of the Thai Gulf, located where the provincial borders of Phetchaburi and Prachuap Khiri Khan meet.

From Phetchaburi, 123 km (76 miles) south-west of Bangkok, to Prachuap Khiri Khan, about 320 km (198 miles) south-west of the capital, Thailand becomes increasingly narrower between western mountains, marking the Thai-Burmese border, and the Thai Gulf.

Phetchaburi, Cha Am and Hua Hin share rich historical association with monarchs of the present Chakri dynasty.

Hua Hin was Thailand's first beachside resort, and has been the Thai royal family's summer residence since King Prajadhipok (reign: 1925–1935) built a palace there called Klai Kangwon (Far From Worries).

HOW TO GET THERE

By Rail
There· are regular rail services from Bangkok, and the journey to Hua Hin takes 4 hours.

By Road
Both resorts can be reached in a comfortable 2.5 hour drive from Bangkok using Route 35 via Samut Songkhram to Pak Tho, and thence south along Highway No. 4.

There are regular coach services from Bangkok.

There are no air services to Cha Am or Hua Hin.

TOURIST INFORMATION
The closest branch of the Tourism Authority of Thailand is their head office in Bangkok, ph 282 1143–7.

ACCOMMODATION

Both Hua Hin and the 'newer' Cha Am have beautifully land-scaped, luxurious beach resort hotels which, complemented by beachside bungalow accommodation, make them ideal venues for family vacations.

Here we have listed just a few examples, and the prices are in bahts for a double room. These should be used as a guide only. The Telephone Area Code is 032.

Regent Cha Am, 849/21 Cha Am Beach, ph 471 483. The hotel has 550 guest rooms spread over five floors and two buildings. Facilities include 4 restaurants, coffee shop, swimming pool, fresh water lake, 4 tennis courts, health club, jogging track and shopping arcade — 1,600–1,800 baht.

Royal Garden Resort Hua Hin, 107/1 Phetkase Beach Road, ph 511 881. The hotel has 222 guest rooms, and the south and north wings are arranged around the swimming pool. There are two restaurants, barbecue terrace and cocktail lounge — 2,780–3,146 baht.

Sofitel, 1 Damnoen Kasem Road, ph 511 012. Formerly known as the Railway Hotel, there are 60 guest rooms, restaurant, swimming pool and tennis court — 1,900–2,200 baht.

Resort Attractions

The popular Cha Am public beach is long, straight and tree-shaded. The narrow beachside road fronts cabins, bungalows and economy-class hotels, shops and numerous restaurants and bars selling simple but delicious seafood.

Cha Am's self-contained resort hotel, The Regent, abuts Gulf waters and its own beach amid landscaped gardens. Tennis, badminton, fishing, windsurfing, sailing and swimming number among popular daytime activities while in-house video programmes, a nightclub, restaurants, bars and a discotheque provide evening entertainment.

Hua Hin's fishing village is separated by a rocky headland from one of Thailand's finest beaches. The beach joins another head-land some 3 km further south where several Buddhist temples cling to rocky hillocks that appear deceptively easy to climb.

The quiet, pine-lined Hat Khao Tao Beach south of this

headland offers great privacy and curves southward to yet another headland and fishing village.

Hotels on Hua Hin's main beach offer pleasant accommodation in a resort which is ideal for doing sweet nothing in tranquil surroundings. The energetic can swim, sail, ride, water-ski, windsurf, parasail, snorkel, fish or play tennis or golf.

Hua Hin retains a genteel 1920s ambience which is best preserved around the beachside Railway Hotel's original wing, which was featured in the award-winning motion picture "The Killing Fields". Polished wooden floors, fin de siecle ceiling fans, decorative teak verandahs and carefully manicured gardens, replete with topiary, belong to another era.

So, too, does Hua Hin's 18-hole golf course which spreads beyond a petite railway station dating from the steam era.

LOCAL TRANSPORT

You have to choose between hiring a car or motorbike, or walking.

EATING OUT AND ENTERTAINMENT

The hotels are your best bet for evening entertainment and dining. There are several good restaurants on Damnoen Kasem Road, near the Sofitel Central Hotel, or if you are into low-brow dining for a change, the central market has excellent seafood.

SHOPPING

Major purchases include local high-quality cottons and silks, readymade sports and leisurewear, preserved seafood such as dried shrimps and squid, and salted fish, preserved fruits and confectionery, and Phetchaburi's famous sweets which include Khanom Mo Kaeng (coconut custard), Khao Kriap (crispy rice) and Foi Thong Krop (crispy golden thread) which are sold with many others in several specialty shops.

SIGHTSEEING

Hua Hin and Cha Am are convenient bases from which to visit major Phetchaburi and Prachuap attractions. Most lie within an hour's journey.

Phetchaburi

Wat Suwannaram
This temple has classic artistic treasures such as an Ayutthayan wooden teaching hall dating from the early 1700s, a three-stilted scriptural repository in the temple pond, and ornate chapel murals.

Khao Luang Caves
They are located just outside town, where late-morning and early-afternoon natural shafts of light illuminate stalactites and Buddha images.

Phra Nakhon Khiri Palace
From the palace a spectacular view of the surrounding countryside may be enjoyed.

Kaeng Krachan National Park
This is Thailand's largest park and has mountainous scenic views. Accommodation overlooking a dam reservoir is available for those wishing to stay a bit longer.

Prachuap

Sam Roi Yot (300 Peaks) National Park
This park occupies more than 60 km^2 (23 sq miles) of coastal land between Pran Buri and Prachuap. Sam Roi Yot was the location for major scenes in "The Killing Fields". Marshland, mangroves and swamps comprise a bird sancturay for numerous species of water-fowl, while caves, beaches, islands, high valleys beckon the explorers.

Prachuap Town
The provincial capital is a fishing town with a scenic bay, bungalow accommodation and the beachside Mirror Mount. A flight of 400 steps on the Mount leads to a small pagoda, chapel and resident monkey tribe. From here there is an excellent view of surrounding sea and countryside.

Suggested 6-Day Itinerary

Day One
Morning departure by road from Bangkok to Phetchabur. Visit Khao Luang Caves, Phra Nakhon Khiri palace, Wat Suwannaram

War Elephant Parade, Surin

Khao Luang Caves, Phetchaburi

Elephant Round-up, Surin

Typical village scene, Northern Thailand

before checking into Cha Am's beachside resort hotel. Overnight stay at Cha Am.

Day Two
Full day of relaxation at Cha Am with option of afternoon exploration of Hua Hin or golf at the resort's 18-hole course. Overnight stay in Cha Am.

Day Three
Morning check-out from Cha Am. Early afternoon check-in at Hua Hin beachside hotel. Afternoon of relaxation, water sports, etc. Overnight stay at Hua Hin.

Day Four
Morning of relaxation, water sports, etc. Afternoon exploration of southern headland, Wat Khao Takiap, Hat Khao Tao Beach, etc. Overnight stay at Hua Hin.

Day Five
Mid-morning departure for Sam Roi Yot National Park. Park exploration and late-afternoon arrival in Prachuap Khiri Khan. Climb Mirror Mount for scenic view. Overnight stay in Prachuap.

Day Six
The traveller has the option of prolonging his stay in Prachuap, travelling onwards to tropical southern Thailand, returning to Hua Hin/Cha Am, or travelling directly to Bangkok.

GOLF
Royal Hua Hin Golf Course, ph 511 099. 6,654 yards, par 72. Open 6am–6pm.
   Green fees — weekdays 150 baht; weekends 250 baht.
   Caddy fee — 100 baht.
   Clubs for hire — 200 baht per day.

Two aspects of the Bridge on the River Kwai

KANCHANABURI

Kanchanaburi is Thailand's fourth largest province, has an area of 19,486 km^2 (7,522 sq miles), and borders Burma to the west of Bangkok.

Kanchanaburi is the site of the world-famous *Bridge over the River Kwai*, and is noted for rugged natural beauty where mountains and river valleys have inspired development of hydro-electric power, and where labyrinthine dam reservoirs add further scenic elements to the province's wild beauty.

Beyond the compact provincial capital, 128 km (79 miles) from Bangkok, the Kwai Yai and Kwai Noi rivers unite to form the Mae Klang river.

HOW TO GET THERE

By Road
Air-conditioned and regular coaches leave Bangkok's Southern Bus Terminal on Charansanitwong Road, ph 414 4978–0 (air) and 411 0511 (regular), throughout the day for the 1.5 hour journey.

By Rail
Trains leave the Bangkok Noi station, ph 411 3102, for the 2.5 hours journey. Yes, it is slower.

There is no air service to Kanchanaburi.

TOURIST INFORMATION
The local office of the Tourism Authority of Thailand is on Saeng Chuto Road, Amphoe Muang, Kanchanaburi, ph (034) 511 200.

ACCOMMODATION
Kanchanaburi offers air-conditioned hotels, bungalows and simple guest houses in the provincial capital. River raft accommodation is available in several rural locations. A current listing of major

accommodation facilities may be obtained from the Tourism Authority of Thailand's Kanchanaburi office.

Here we have included a couple of hotels, with the prices in bahts for a double room per night. These should be used as a guide only. The Telephone Area Code is 034.

River Kwai Hotel, 284/3-16 Saeng Chuto Road, Amphoe Muang, ph 511 184 — 127 guest rooms — bar, coffee shop, swimming pool, videotheque, disco and shopping arcade — 644–944 baht.

River Kwai Village, 72 Mu 4, Amphoe Soi Yak, ph Bangkok 251 7828 — 60 guest rooms and 28 raft (houseboat) accommodation — restaurant, bar, coffee shop, swimming pool, videotheque and shopping arcade — 750–850 baht.

LOCAL TRANSPORT
There is a local bus service. Enquire at the Tourism Authority office for details. As the main attraction here is the River Kwai, there are local tours to show you the sights, or you can hire a taxi, or rent a car and be independent.

EATING OUT AND ENTERTAINMENT
The hotels are the main source of night time activities. This area is not really known for its nightlife.

There is a floating restaurant beside the River Kwai Bridge.

SHOPPING
This is not really a great area for general shopping. Of course, near the Bridge there are several souvenir shops, and also jewellery shops which sell prized blue sapphires mined in the Bo Phloi area about 50 km (30 miles) north of town.

SIGHTSEEING
The provincial capital's major attractions are connected with World War II.

Foremost among them is the already mentioned world-famous Bridge over the River Kwai, the subject of a popular motion picture and several books. The bridge was constructed by Allied prisoner-of-war labour, under Japanese supervision, as part of the 'Death Railway' linking Siam and Burma.

The bridge, still in use today, was a target of frequent Allied bombing raids during 1945 and is featured in an annual Light and Sound presentation each December during the River Kwai Bridge Week when events connected with the area are re-enacted.

A small Railway Museum at the bridge's eastern approach features steam locomotives and a peculiar road/railcar from that era.

A Japanese War Memorial occupies riverside land just south of the bridge, and three kilometres away, inland near the railway station, the Kanchanaburi War Cemetery is the largest of two Allied war cemeteries where 6,982 bodies are interred in peaceful, immaculately maintained surroundings.

The second cemetery, Chongkai, 2 km south of town on the west bank of the Kwai Noi river, occupies the former site of the Chongkai Prisoner of War Camp, and contains some 1,750 graves.

A War Museum in the riverside precincts of Wat Chaichumphon has been constructed in the form of a prisoner-of-war camp, and contains photographic, pictorial and physical memorabilia from the Second World War.

Incidentally, the local pronunciation of Kwai is 'Kwey'.

Other city attractions include Wat Tham Mangkhon Thong cave monastery.

OUTLYING ATTRACTIONS

Essentially, there are two land routes for exploring Kanchanaburi's major attractions.

The more western Route 323 largely parallels the Kwai Noi river to the Khao Laem Dam reservoir, while Route 3199 follows the Kwai Yai river to Si Nakharin Dam.

Along Route 323

15 km (9 miles)	—	Phu Phra Cave, where a legendary character from Thai literature is said to have studied magic.
35 km (22 miles)	—	Ban Kao Museum which contains skeletal remains and artefacts of prehistoric man.

37 km (23 miles)	—	Wang Takhian Cave.
43 km (27 miles)	—	Khmer Prasat Muang Sing (Tower of the City of Lions). This was the 12th century westernmost outpost of the Angkor-centred Khmer empire.
60 km (37 miles)	—	Saiyok Noi or Khao Phang Waterfall.
75 km (46 miles)	—	Lawa Cave has stalactites and stalagmites in several chambers.
104 km (64 miles)	—	Saiyok Yai Waterfall has been repeatedly celebrated in ancient Thai songs and poetry. It is the focal point of a riverside national park with popular raft accommodation.
110 km (68 miles)	—	Daowadung Cave.
130 km (81 miles)	—	Hin Dat Hot Springs.
140 km (87 miles)	—	Pha Tat Waterfall (12 km — 7 miles — north-east of Route 323).
153 km (95 miles)	—	Khao Laem Dam.
241 km (146 miles)	—	Three Pagodas Pass at the Thai-Burmese border, and the remote Thung Yai Sanctuary Park. Travel to such areas demands 4WD vehicles. Visitors wishing to do so should check road conditions with the Tourism Authority's local office.
Along Route 3199	—	*detour along Route 3086*
48 km (30 miles)	—	Bo Phloi, where the blue sapphires are mined.
97 km (60 miles)	—	Than Lot Cave and Traitrung Waterfall in the Than Lot National Park.
Along Route 3199		
65 km (40 miles)	—	Erawan National Park and seven-tiered Erawan Waterfall.
69 km (43 miles)	—	Si Nakharin Dam.
76 km (47 miles)	—	Phra That Cave, on the dam's western shore.
108 km (67 miles)	—	Huai Khamin Waterfall.

From Kanchanaburi, returning to Bangkok along Route 324 via Suphanburi, you can visit the Don Chedi memorial where a white pagoda and statue of Ayutthaya's King Naresuan the Great astride a war elephant marks the king's victory, at that spot, in single combat on elephants, over the Burmese Crown Prince in 1592.

Suggested 7-Day Itinerary

Day One
Morning departure by road from Bangkok. Visit Samphran Crocodile Farm, Nakhon Pathom, proceed to Kanchanaburi. Check-in to hotel. Dinner at floating restaurant beside River Kwai Bridge. Overnight stay in Kanchanaburi.

Day Two
Morning visit to Allied War Cemetery, War Museum, Bridge and Railway Museum. Afternoon visit to Prasat Muang Sing and/or Ban Kao Museum. Overnight stay in Kanchanaburi.

Day Three
Full-day trip to Bo Phloi and Than Lot National Park. Overnight stay in Kanchanaburi.

Day Four
Full-day trip to Erawan National Park, Si Nakharin Dam, Phra That Cave and Huai Khamin Waterfall. Overnight stay in Kanchanaburi.

Day Five
Check-out of hotel. Visit Khao Phang Waterfall, proceed to Pak Saeng Pier, enjoy 2.5 hour boat trip to Lawa Cave and Saiyok Yai Waterfall. Overnight stay on Saiyok river raft or at River Kwai Village Hotel.

Day Six
Visit Hin Dat Hot Springs, Pha Tat Waterfall, Khao Laem Dam, return to Kanchanaburi for an overnight stay.

Day Seven
Morning departure, either to Damnoen Saduak Floating Market, and Rose Garden for afternoon show, or to Suphanburi and Don Chedi memorial, before late-afternoon arrival in Bangkok.

NAKHON RATCHASIMA

Nakhon Ratchasima, Thailand's seventh most populous city, is capital of Thailand's second largest province. More popularly known as Khorat, it dates from the mid–1600s and lies 259 km (160 miles) north-east of Bangkok.

The Gateway to North-East Thailand and the north-east plateau which contains 17 of Thailand's 73 provinces, Nakhon Ratchasima is a thriving commercial and entertainment centre.

HOW TO GET THERE

By Air
Bangkok Airways operate 3 daily 35-minute flights between Bangkok and Khorat, ph 253 4014–5 for details.

By Rail
There are daily rail services from Bangkok to Nakhon Ratchasima, and railway schedules can be obtained from Bangkok's Hualampong Station, ph 223 7461. The trip takes 5 hours.

By Bus
Air-conditioned and regular coaches leave Bangkok's Northern/North-eastern Bus Terminal on Phahonyothin Road, ph 279 4484–7 (air) and 279 6222 (regular). The road journey takes 4 hours.

TOURIST INFORMATION

The local office of the Tourism Authority of Thailand is at 2102–2104 Mittraphap Road, Tambon Nai Muang, Amphoe Muang, ph (044) 243 427, 243 751.

ACCOMMODATION

There are several first-class and economy-class hotels with air-conditioned facilities. A comprehensive list of current accommodation can be obtained from the local office of the Tourism Authority of Thailand.

Here we have listed a few, with prices in bahts for a double room per night, which should be used as a guide only. The Telephone Area Code is 044.

Chomsurang Hotel, 2701/1-2 Mahadthai Road, Amphoe Muang, ph 257 088. There are 119 guest rooms, a restaurant, swimming pool, disco and shopping arcade — 500 baht.

Khao Yai Motor Lodge, Amphoe Pak Chong, ph Bangkok 281 3041. Accommodation is in bungalows, and there is a restaurant — 450–550 baht.

Muang Mai Korat, 191 At-Sadang Road, Amphoe Muang, ph 242 260. 115 guest rooms, coffee shop, disco and shopping arcade — 320 baht (for air-conditioned room).

Sripatana, 346 Suranaree Road, Amphoe Muang, ph 255 372. There are 183 guest rooms, a bar, coffee shop, swimming pool and shopping arcade — 350 baht.

Srivichai, 9-11 Boarong Road, Amphoe Muang, ph 242 194. A smaller hotel with 57 guest rooms, a restaurant, coffee shop and disco — 170–250 baht.

EATING OUT AND ENTERTAINMENT
Khorat's nightlife is concentrated mainly around the major hotels and bars. Specialty restaurants and eating places are centred in Chumphon, Ratchadamnoen and Buarong Road.

SHOPPING
Major shopping areas, for Takthongchai silk, Ban Dan Kwian ceramics and local culinary delicacies, including spicy sausages and preserves, are Chumphon, Chakkri and Manat Roads.

Khorat's major handicrafts are silk-weaving and ceramics. Silk-weaving can be seen at the Pakthongchai Silk Weaving Village, 32 km (20 miles) south of Khorat. Silk lengths and materials can be purchased.

Ceramics can be found at Ban Dan Kwian, 15 km (9 miles) south-east of Khorat on Highway No. 24, where local villagers have created decorative items for home and garden, including tiles and jewellery. Their roadside display fronts a fascinating collection of traditional farming implements and carts.

SIGHTSEEING

Thao Suranari Memorial
At Chumphon Gate in the heart of the city, the statue-cum-shrine of the local and national heroine, Khunying Mo, commemorates her exploits in 1826 when she rallied the townspeople to repel invaders from Vientiane.

Wat Sala Loi
Located in the north-east part of town is Khorat's best-known temple, and features an unusual chapel surrounded by ornamental ponds.

Somdet Maha Wirawong Museum
The branch of the National Museum is in the compound of Suthachinda temple on Ratchadamnoen Road, and displays Khmer and Thai objects d'art including Buddha images, earthern-ware and woodcarvings.

Silver Lake
A water park, featuring colourful water slides, shaded pools and ornamental gardens, located near the TAT office on Mukkha-montri Road.

OUTLYING ATTRACTIONS
Nakhon Ratchasima's major man-made attractions are the various Khmer prasat hin temples scattered throughout the area, a legacy of north-east Thailand's former importance to the Angkor-centred Khmer empire.

Phimai
In this town the 11th century Prasat Hin is the largest example of classical Khmer architecture outside Kampuchea. It lies about 60 km (37 miles) north of Khorat along Highway No. 2 and Route 206.

The temple occupies land within boundary walls measuring 250 by 280 m (272.5 by 305 yds), and was sufficiently important to have been connected by road with Angkor, Kampuchea.

Nearby, the Fine Arts Department Regional Office No. 6 displays lintels and sanctuary carvings from other nearby Khmer monuments.

At Sai Ngam, about 2 km outside Phimai, there is Thailand's largest banyan tree.

Lesser prasat hin temples are found at Khorakhapura, about 30 km (19 miles) west of Khorat, and Prasat Hin Wat Phanomwan, 21 km (13 miles) north of Khorat.

Khao Yai National Park

Thailand's second largest, this park spreads across Khorat, Saraburi, Nakhon Nayok and Prachinburi provinces at an average elevation of 800 m (2,600 ft). The park's highest peak is 1,328 m (4,316 ft). The park has an area of 218,623 ha (540,000 acres).

Khao Yai supports a great variety of protected wildlife, including tigers, elephants, deer, monkeys, bears, wild oxen, silver pheasants, woodpeckers, great hornbills and numerous butterfly species. There are also countless species of wild flowers, orchids and trees. It is laced with hiking trails and has 10 beautiful waterfalls.

The park also possesses Thailand's highest golf course, comfortable motor lodge accommodation, restaurant, camping and wildlife-watching facilities.

For naturalists, or indeed anyone interested in flora and fauna, a 2 to 5-day stay at Khao Yai can be very rewarding.

Suggested 5-Day Itinerary

Day One
Travel by road from Bangkok via Hin Kong and Nakhon Nayok to Khao Yai National Park. Afternoon visit to popular Heo Suwat waterfall.

Evening — 'wildlife safari' with spotlights to sight deer, elephants, etc.

Overnight stay at Khao Yai.

Day Two
Morning round of golf on Thailand's highest course/explore local waterfalls/wildlife-watching with help of local wardens.

Overnight stay at Khao Yai.

Day Three
Morning departure, via Pak Chong, along Highway No. 2 for Khorat. Visit ancient towns of Sema and Khorakhapura before

entering Khorat. Afternoon visit to 11th century prasat hin temples of Wat Phanomwan and Phimai.

Overnight stay in Khorat.

Day Four

Morning trip to Buriram's hilltop Phanom Rung Khmer temple and Ban Dan Kwian to inspect ceramic handicrafts. Afternoon relaxation at Silver Lake water park.

Overnight stay in Khorat.

Day Five

Morning visit to Wat Sala Loi, Thao Suranari Memorial, Somdet Maha Wirawong Museum. Afternoon flight to Bangkok, or travel onwards to other north-east destinations.

GOLF

Khao Yai Golf Course, 2,980 yards, par 36 (nine holes). Contact address is the Tourism Authority of Thailand, Ratchadamnoen Nok Avenue, Bangkok, ph 282 1143–7.

Open 6am–6pm. Accommodation available — 380–900 baht per person per night.

Green fees — weekday 80 baht, weekends 140 baht.

Caddy fee — 80 baht for 18 holes.

Clubs for hire — 200 baht.

LIST OF MAPS

INDEX